DIDSBURY LECTURES 2002

JOHN WESLEY

REVD HERBERT B MCGONIGLE

MA BD DD PHD

Former Lecturer at Nazarene Theological College, Dene Road, Didsbury, Manchester, in the classes in Church History, Theology and Wesley Studies, Former Principal of Nazarene Theological College for 18 years and now Principal Emeritus.

British Library Cataloguing in Publication Data.
A catalogue record for this book is available from the British Library

ISBN 978 0 86071 817 8

Contents

Foreword

Foreword [to the Rev Dr Herbert McGonigle's 2002 Didsbury Lectures: 'To Know One Thing']

Just like some examples in John Wesley's day, this foreword (with its appendix) is of an extraordinarily long length. Even though there may be some interest to be found in it, if your time is limited, please ignore the appendix (for now at least!) and proceed to the printed words of Dr McGonigle, now published for the first time in this book. They are the very words he used verbatim when he delivered his four Didsbury lectures to an audience in Manchester in 2002. I was a member of that audience and the clarity and content of the lecturer's words then gripped my attention right through the four evenings – just as they can still do for me today, around eighteen years later. So I can certainly recommend the content of these four lectures unreservedly for you to read, too! They speak of profound issues arising, through God's grace, from John Wesley's five or more decades of body-and-soul-saving work in the eighteenth century, but they also have an underlying 'on fire' message for anyone today living in the midst of the breath-taking opportunities and challenges of the twenty-first century.

At the beginning of his first lecture, Dr McGonigle informs us that he has adopted as his overall title for the four lectures John Wesley's own words, 'To Know One Thing'.[1] By doing this he is emphasising at the outset that Christian soteriology – the salvation of souls through Christ's work at Calvary – as revealed in the Bible, was the compelling focus of Wesley's theology and life's work, and by implication that it is also that of the lecturer himself. So go for it, and begin reading these lectures! Their uncluttered clarity will not disappoint you. Just one further thought, as a matter of personal choice, I have found that a particularly enjoyable way to read the words of these lectures has been to do it simultaneously whilst listening to recordings made as Dr McGonigle actually delivered the lectures in 2002. If

---

[1] John Wesley had written: '. . . I want to know one thing, the way to heaven . . . . God . . . hath written it down in a book. O give me that book!', and first published this statement in the definitive preface to the first volume of his collected sermons: *Sermons on Several Occasions: in Three Volumes*, London: Printed by W. Strahan, 1746; reprinted many times since, including in: Albert C. Outler, ed., *The Works of John Wesley*, Bicentennial Edition, Nashville: Abingdon Press, 1984, Vol. 1, p. 105.

you wanted to try this method for yourself, you can find how this can be done by checking through my musings in the 'Foreword Appendix' below, which attempts to give more information about the background to the lectures and the lecturer!
Bill Graham
Manchester, 9 January 2020

Appendix to Foreword [By William T Graham, Jan 2020]

The notion of establishing an annual Didsbury Lecture series of high academic quality was first mooted by the Nazarene College in Didsbury, Manchester, in the late 1970s. The intention was to establish a significant platform in the conurbation to which leading thinkers from within the historic Christian faith, and usually resident in the United Kingdom, might be invited to address a topic of contemporary relevance of their own choosing, selected from the area of knowledge traditionally known by the term 'Divinity'.

By the late 1990s the series had become well-established with a growing interest reaching beyond just the United Kingdom of Great Britain and Northern Ireland. As the College had its roots in the Wesleyan theological tradition, the committee responsible for the Lectures well understood they would need to respond to a forthcoming momentous anniversary year for Methodism. This was the tercentenary of the birth of John Wesley, who had been born at Epworth, Lincolnshire in June 1703. Even the British parliament was roused to acknowledge the merit of the occasion, recognising Wesley as 'the renowned preacher and a leader of the "Methodist" eighteenth century revival' which 'led to a significant and lasting contribution to the awakening of spiritual and social values in individuals and communities throughout the world'[2]. Realising the 2002 Didsbury Lectures would be a precursor to this significant tercentenary year, it was decided to adjust the 'rules' and nominate not just the speaker (the Revd Dr Herbert McGonigle), but also the subject ('John Wesley').

---

[2] See the House of Commons 'Early Day Motion' of congratulations to the Methodist Church tabled 17 June 2003 at https://edm.parliament.uk/early-day-motion/22469/tercentenary-of-birth-of-john-wesley (accessed December 2019).

McGonigle had been a full-time lecturer at the College since 1976[3], and Principal since 1986, so his long interest in and knowledge of the Wesleys and their work was well understood - not only to students but to many others beyond the College who had read some of his publications[4], or known him as a fellow scholar, colleague, lecturer, pastor or preacher. So it was not a surprise that the audience chuckled when Herbert, at the beginning of his first Didsbury lecture, claimed to have 'played no part' in the choice of lecturer, or the subject of 'John Wesley'. The mirth was generated not because anyone questioned the veracity of his word, but simply because there was no doubt in their minds that the Committee would have been lacking in common sense if they had not invited Dr McGonigle. It was clearly accepted that, although he was a member of their own institution, there was probably no other Wesley scholar worldwide who was better qualified for this task than the Principal. So it was that Dr McGonigle became, in 2002, the first member of the College faculty actually serving in post to be invited as a Didsbury Lecturer.

To measure the honour placed on Herbert McGonigle by this invitation one has only to remember that he was following a distinguished line of 23 former Didsbury Lecturers, each and all of whom were widely acknowledged as outstanding scholars of international repute. The standard had been set at the highest level when the inaugural Didsbury Lecture was given in 1979 by the renowned theologian and scholar, the late F.F. Bruce (then a Fellow of the British Academy, and The Rylands Professor of Biblical Criticism and Exegesis at the University of Manchester). Bruce had been followed by other highly regarded scholars - such as the late Revd Dr I. Howard Marshall (then Professor of New Testament Exegesis at the University of Aberdeen); the Rev Prof Morna D Hooker (then Lady Margaret's Professor of Divinity within the University of Cambridge). And the list goes on down the years with other notable scholars up to 2001, when Robert P. Gordon (then a Fellow of the British Academy, and Regius Professor of Hebrew at the University of Cambridge and a Professorial Fellow of St Catharine's College, Cambridge) was the Didsbury Lecturer in the year immediately preceding Herbert McGonigle.

---

[3] Prior to that, and following graduation from the Nazarene College in Manchester in 1960, he had been an effective and much loved pastor at Nazarene churches at Walthamstow, London; Uddingston, Glasgow; and Dewsbury Road, Leeds.

[4] For details of some of his publications see below for the section entitled: 'Herbert McGonigle, A Selected Bibliography of his Writings'.

So the writer of this Forcword realises it is a distinct privilege, even if an undeserved honour, to have been invited by Dr McGonigle to write these introductory words to this his latest volume, based on his four 2002 Didsbury Lectures. It is an apparent undeserved honour simply because Herbert is recognised globally as an eminent Wesley scholar[5], and a notable 'historian of holiness',[6] whose academic achievements and scholarship can easily stand alongside other distinguished men and women who have also been Didsbury Lecturers. A further reason for questioning the honour placed on the writer is that such a foreword really demands an equally scholarly introduction to these 2002 lectures. This argument is further intensified when it is remembered that the lecture series has now grown to not only become a significant event in the United Kingdom's theological calendar, but through their printed publication (and more recently also live streaming on the Internet) the annual Didsbury Lectures now reach a global audience.

It may be true that the writer of this foreword was present when Dr McGonigle originally delivered his lectures on those four consecutive evenings during the autumn of 2002 to a crowded audience in the J B Maclagan Chapel, at Nazarene Theological College, Didsbury, Manchester (NTC). But such attendance alone can hardly qualify one to write this foreword! After all, there were distinguished Wesley scholars present in the audience then, and many others since, who would have been able to provide a far more erudite introduction to these lectures. The honour is so great that one might even have been tempted to flatter oneself by echoing Shakespeare's words in *Twelfth Night*: 'Some are born great, some achieve greatness, and some have greatness thrust upon them'! But surely Dr McGonigle's reason for his magnanimous invitation is of a kind best revealed in the kindly humour of John Newton (the former slave-ship master, celebrated abolitionist and Church of England clergyman) who, in his letter to John Wesley on 14 November 1760 wonders, and writes: 'Reverend and dear Sir, How shall I thank you, for the obliging notice you take of me? . . .

---

[5] In a recent *Festschrift* in his honour Dr McGonigle is described as being 'Recognized internationally for his expertise in Wesley Studies', see: Joseph Cunningham and David Rainey, eds., *The Path of Holiness: Perspectives in Wesleyan Thought in Honor of Herbert B. McGonigle*, Lexington, Kentucky: Emeth Press, 2014, p. 1.

[6] See: David Bebbington, *Holiness in Nineteenth-Century England: The 1998 Didsbury Lectures*, Carlisle: Paternoster Press, 2000, p. v.

In one sense only, I think myself not altogether unworthy of your friendship; that is, I am not ungrateful.'[7]

Yes, I am indeed 'not ungrateful' to Herbert for his (and his late wife Jeanne's) friendship over more than forty years, because it has given me this opportunity to comment not so much on the detailed *content* of the lectures (I shall leave that to others better qualified to do so!) but more on briefly mentioning a few examples of the many other achievements, under God's grace, of the *man* who delivered these lectures in 2002, as well as offering an explanation for why it has taken nearly eighteen years for them to appear in print. The motto now has been, 'better late than not at all'!

It might be appropriate at this point to comment on the actual text of these four lectures as now finally published. At some time after 2002 Dr McGonigle's original digital copy of the text was lost in an unfortunate computer disaster. As there was no digital backup, this necessitated a new digital copy having to be made from the original paper lecture notes. I have not seen the *final* version of the text that Dr McGonigle has since worked on ready for publication. So it remains possible that various typographical changes or slips may have crept into this text from what was originally written. The good news is that the original words spoken by Dr McGonigle when he gave the four lectures in 2002 were recorded.[8] So it is possible for anyone who so desires to at least *hear* what was said at the time, and compare that with the text now available in print. The original written text might well have been considerably extended by Dr McGonigle not long after 2002 if matters had worked out differently, as explained below. Although some may feel this to be a loss, the plain original lecture notes as now printed have the advantages of a brevity and clarity of thought which is well able to convey to a reader the essence of the message delivered in the spoken lectures in 2002.

---

[7] First published by John Wesley (ed.) in *The Arminian Magazine*, Vol. 3, Aug. 1780, pp. 441-2.

[8] The Archives at Nazarene Theological College, Manchester, hold audio recordings on four CDs of the Rev Dr Herbert McGonigle delivering his 2002 Didsbury Lectures, 'To Know One Thing', namely: CD:01, 'John Wesley and Scripture'; CD:02, 'John Wesley and Prevenient Grace'; CD:03, 'John Wesley and Salvation'; and CD:04, 'John Wesley and Evangelism'. They are not high definition recordings, but they are clear and audible. Further details of how to access or purchase these recordings can be obtained by contacting the NTC Archivist at archives@nazarene.ac.uk

The delay in publication has arisen by accident rather than design. At the time when Dr McGonigle delivered the lectures he made the decision to work on his notes at a later date, and hopefully then have more time to prepare a more substantial text on the life and work of John Wesley. He made the decision partly because he was then much engaged not only on his work as Principal at NTC (with related additional responsibilities as Senior Lecturer in Church History and Senior Lecturer in Wesley Studies, supervision of some doctoral research students, various preaching and lecturing engagements worldwide - not to mention some voluntary pastoral support at the Salford Church of the Nazarene where he and his wife were then members, or the work as Chairman of the then flourishing Wesley Fellowship). But more to the immediate point, Herbert was now *also* very heavily involved in preparing for two important and significant events that were due to take place in 2003.

One of these tasks was Herbert's time-consuming preparatory committee work for the forthcoming residential international conference, 'John Wesley: Life, Legend, and Legacy', to be held at the University of Manchester in June 2003 to mark the tercentenary of Wesley's birth. This brought together nearly 200 delegates from all over the world, with historians, theologians, and specialists in literature and language presenting over fifty individual papers (one of whom, for example, was Dr Thomas A Noble, also of NTC, with his 'East and West in the theology of John Wesley'). The conference was a productive collaboration between the John Rylands Library and the University of Manchester's Department of Religions and Theology. The numerous conference sponsors included several Nazarene institutions from around the world, and Dr McGonigle himself was noted as an important 'hard-working member' of the Conference Organising Committee, of what was later acknowledged to have been 'the major international academic event' of its kind during the year 2003.[9]

Also in 2003, another momentous event in which Herbert McGonigle was both influential and heavily involved was the inauguration of the Manchester Wesley Research Centre (MWRC). This took place when documents were signed, by a range of partners involved, during the afternoon of Wednesday

---

[9] Jeremy Gregory, ed., 'John Wesley: Tercentenary Essays. Proceedings of a Conference held at the University of Manchester, June 2003', in: *Bulletin of the John Rylands University Library of Manchester*, Vol. 85, Numbers 2 and 3, Summer and Autumn 2003, p. 8.

18 June 2003 in the J B Maclagan Chapel at NTC. This was a sequel to and immediately following the final morning plenary session of the 'John Wesley: Life, Legend, and Legacy' Conference. Indeed, numerous delegates took up the invitation to travel from the university to the Nazarene college to be present at the inauguration.[10] The charter signatories to the partnership composing the MWRC were: NTC; the University of Manchester John Rylands Library; the University of Manchester Department of Religions and Theology; the International Board of Education of the Church of the Nazarene; and the Nazarene Theological Seminary (Kansas City, Missouri). Dr McGonigle was appointed as the first Director of the MWRC in 2003 (a position he held until his retirement in 2010, when he became MWRC Director Emeritus; Dr McGonigle had resigned as Principal of NTC in 2004, and is now NTC Principal Emeritus).

The MWRC was established to promote research scholarship in: 'the life and work of John and Charles Wesley; their contemporaries in the Eighteenth Century Revival; their historical and theological antecedents; and contemporary scholarship within the Wesleyan and Evangelical tradition'. The establishment of the MWRC at the NTC campus in Didsbury has highlighted to scholars around the world[11] the attractive 'hands-on' availability of the magnificent resources of the Methodist Archives which are housed within the University of Manchester John Rylands Library and within easy travelling distance from the NTC Didsbury campus. Herbert McGonigle's pioneering contribution to the establishment of this growing and developing research facility must be one of the most significant legacies he has left to academia.[12]

---

[10] One of these delegates was Dr Kenneth J. Collins, Professor of Historical Theology and Wesley Studies at Asbury Theological Seminary, Wilmore, Kentucky, USA, who having met Dr McGonigle at NTC and seen what resources MWRC would have to offer research students, intimated that he would urge Asbury to join as one of its Institutional Partners.

[11] Some of whom first met Dr McGonigle and became interested in the project during the 2003 'John Wesley: Life, Legend, and Legacy' Conference at the University of Manchester.

[12] For details of the growing number of world-wide institutions now partners in the MWRC under the current Directorship of Dr Geordan Hammond, see http://www.mwrc.ac.uk/partnerships/ (accessed Dec 2019).

A glance at the bibliographies at the end of this appendix will soon show that for more than five decades beginning in the 1960s, Herbert McGonigle has been publishing a variety of numerous articles designed for different audiences. So he wrote mainly for scholars in journals such as the *Wesleyan Theological Journal*; and for pastors and preachers in periodicals such as the *Nazarene Preacher* or the *Preacher's Magazine*. For much of this time he was also a member of the Editorial Board of the Revd Maynard James' magazine *The Flame* (and for a time also Associate Editor); and one of the bibliographies below shows that in *The Flame* some of his articles were aimed at children, although most were designed to interest and encourage lay people in the Christian faith.

Another aspect of Herbert McGonigle's work had been the establishment of The Wesley Fellowship (WF) which held regular meetings twice a year from about 1985-2015.[13] The idea of such an organisation can be traced back to 1983 and discussions between Herbert McGonigle and the Revd Dr William Parkes, then a Methodist Superintendent Minister (and sometime Councillor and Mayor) in Biddulph, Staffordshire. By 1985, following encouragement from several scholars[14], particularly the Rev Dr Arthur Skevington Wood[15] (who was to become its first Hon. President), the Wesley Fellowship was formally established as an 'international and interdenominational fellowship of Christians committed to the spirit and teaching of John and Charles Wesley', and 'seeking to make relevant in this present age the distinctive doctrines of the historic Wesleyan expressions of faith.' An executive committee (under the Chairmanship of Herbert McGonigle and Vice-Chairmanship of William Parkes) was formed and meetings with invited

---

[13] Details of some of the original work of the Wesley Fellowship up to about 2014 can still be seen on its now largely inactive and 'fossilised' website at https://www.wesley-fellowship.org.uk/ (accessed Dec. 2019).

[14] One was the retired Methodist minister, Revd John Lawson, then of Exeter, a member from the 1970s of the Editorial Board of the Oxford Edition of Wesley's Works, later the Bicentennial Edition. For an obituary see *Wesley Fellowship Quarterly*, Dec. 2003.

[15] Following Skevington Wood's death in 1993, the Wesley Fellowship sponsored a book about him, namely: Paul Taylor and Howard Mellor, eds, *Travelling Man: A tribute to the Life and Ministry of the Reverend Dr Arthur Skevington Wood*, Ilkeston: Moorleys Print & Publishing, 1994. This book also contains a reprint of the very first publication (in 1986) of the Wesley Fellowship, which was Dr Wood's significant paper, read to the WF's inaugural meeting in Sheffield, entitled: *Love Excluding Sin: Wesley's doctrine of Sanctification*.

speakers were held in the spring and autumn, plus occasional residential conferences instead of the usual autumn meeting. The membership for a time reached well over 200, and meetings often attracted more than fifty persons. The WF was active for more than a quarter of a century but by 2014, having failed to attract many younger persons, over time the attendance at meetings had dropped significantly - mainly due to infirmity, old age and deaths of regular members. The Executive decided it was best to organise no more meetings, concluding that for more than a quarter of a century the fellowship had served its purpose and run its course.

Nevertheless, even a glance below at the bibliography entitled 'Publications associated directly or indirectly with the Wesley Fellowship' will show that the Wesley Fellowship in one way or another led to over sixty worthwhile interesting and informative publications being produced, working out as an average of more than two for each year of its existence. Those persons who were fortunate enough to attend these meetings found many blessings from the friendly Christian fellowship and the interchange of ideas. There were wonderful opportunities to learn from face-to-face meetings, often with inspiring scholars of international repute who had been invited to speak at meetings[16] – with a chance to ask questions either in the meeting or later more informally when having refreshments together. The WF residential conferences also gave more time and so offered opportunities for times of worship, 'Love Feasts', singing Wesleyan hymns, and preaching, as well as occasional visits to places of 'Wesleyan' interest, such as to the New Room in Bristol.

Herbert McGonigle himself brought numerous papers to meetings of the Wesley Fellowship, and the bibliography below, entitled 'Publications associated directly or indirectly with the Wesley Fellowship', provides the titles of those that were published or sponsored by the Fellowship. Most of these published papers have the advantage of being readable, short in length

---

[16] Herbert McGonigle was often able to arrange for notable Wesley scholars who happened to be visiting Britain from abroad for other events, to *also* speak at WF meetings, notable examples being: Dr Paul M. Bassett, who was then Professor of the History of Christianity, at Nazarene Theological Seminary, Kansas City, Missouri, USA; and Dr William M. Greathouse (1919-2011) who at the time (1989) was a General Superintendent in the Church of the Nazarene and previously had been president of Nazarene Theological Seminary in Kansas City, Missouri.

and yet dealing with important aspects of Wesleyan history and theology, together with a message applicable to the challenges facing a Christian living in the contemporary world of today.

All these activities, responsibilities, together with Herbert's preaching and speaking engagements around the globe[17] meant that for year-after-year following 2003, Dr McGonigle needed to put to one side his personal desire to expand his Didsbury lectures into a greatly enlarged work on the subject of John Wesley. Then, without warning in 2009, all such plans came to an abrupt halt when Herbert suffered a serious stroke which led to his retirement as Director of the MWRC. Over time since then Herbert has gradually regained some of his writing powers, and a glance below, particularly to the 'Selected Bibliography of his Writings', and the 'asterisked' items from No. 74 onwards, it can be seen that Herbert has been able (since 2014) to start publishing a range of attractive booklets on a range of interesting 'Wesleyan connected' subjects.[18]

Another of these 'legacies' came to light in August 2019, when Herbert Boyd Quinton Adams McGonigle celebrated his eightieth birthday.[19] He was

---

[17] Examples include invitations to Japan, South Korea and the United States; as well as in the UK, to events such as the Methodist Conference at Loughborough to give the 2004 Wesley Historical Society Annual Lecture, 'William Bramwell: A Re-Appraisal', or to Tyndale House and Fellowship in Cambridge in 2005 to present his paper 'Christianity or Deism? John Wesley's Response to John Taylor's Denial of the Doctrine of Original Sin'.

[18] Strictly speaking these are private 'publications', printed in small numbers, not put on sale, and mainly given as gifts to Dr McGonigle's personal friends. Some are ostensibly new works, others are based on writing that Herbert had worked on before his stroke. Generally, these post-2014 works are best classified as of a different genre to his 'pre-stroke' writings. The effort to produce them has had clear therapeutic benefits for Herbert and brought spiritual delight to his readers.

[19] Herbert Boyd Quinton Adams McGonigle (his full name as recorded on his birth certificate) was born on Tuesday 15 August 1939 at the family farm at Mullanachose, near Stranorlar, Co. Donegal, Ulster, Ireland – although the family moved, while Herbert was still a schoolboy, to live at another farm in Co. Fermanagh, Northern Ireland. Herbert's given name of 'Quinton' is from the maiden surname of his mother, Lucy Ledia Quinton (1902-1994); and his given name of 'Adams' is from the maiden surname of his paternal-grandmother, Elizabeth Adams (c. 1862-1909). The McGonigle family have no known ancestors or blood relations who have the name 'Herbert' or 'Boyd'.

astonished to be informed, and then shown (by colleagues from NTC visiting him) that he was mentioned on 'social media' – an area of the Internet completely unfamiliar to Herbert. His astonishment turned to delight as he began reading (on the Facebook account of the college where he is Principal Emeritus) seemingly countless congratulations and expressions of gratitude from his former students and others from around the world – each of whom had benefited from his teaching and ministry. Comments – such as: 'a wonderful man and tutor'; 'blessed and inspired by your teaching'; 'an inspiration to so many of us'; 'a great encourager to me'; and 'a talented Godly man' – all gave testimony to the affection and esteem so many people have for the way Herbert McGonigle has helped them and influenced their lives academically, and for Christ.

....

HERBERT MCGONIGLE, A SELECTED BIBLIOGRAPHY OF HIS WRITINGS, PREPARED BY WILLIAM T GRAHAM:

1. Herbert McGonigle, "The Essentials of Success", *Nazarene Preacher*, Vol. 41, No. 11, November 1966, pp 7-9; accessed Jan 2017 at < http://digitalcommons.olivet.edu/cgi/viewcontent.cgi?article=1472&context=cotn_pm >
2. Herbert McGonigle, "Studies in the Methodist Revival: Part I, Conversion: John and Charles Wesley", *Nazarene Preacher*, March 1967, pp 14-18; accessed Jan 2016 at < http://digitalcommons.olivet.edu/cgi/viewcontent.cgi?article=1476&context=cotn_pm >
3. Herbert McGonigle, "Studies in the Methodist Revival: Part II, The Methodist Pentecost", *Nazarene Preacher*, Vol. 42, No. 4, April 1967, pp 8-12; accessed Jan 2016 at < http://digitalcommons.olivet.edu/cgi/viewcontent.cgi?article=1477&context=cotn_pm >
4. Herbert McGonigle, "Studies in the Methodist Revival: Part III, The Calvinistic Controversy in Early Methodism", *Nazarene Preacher*, Vol. 42, No. 5, May 1967, pp. 5-10; accessed Jan 2017 < http://digitalcommons.olivet.edu/cgi/viewcontent.cgi?article=1478&context=cotn_pm >
5. Herbert McGonigle, "When St Paul Crossed the Hellespont", *Preacher's Magazine*, Vol. 44, No. 12, December 1969, pp 4-6; accessed March 2014

at <
http://digitalcommons.olivet.edu/cgi/viewcontent.cgi?article=1509&context=cotn_pm>

6. Herbert McGonigle, 'William Bramwell' [Do we ask the difference between holiness evangelism and any other kind? Study Bramwell, and we will know.], *Nazarene Preacher*, Vol. 46, No. 3, March 1971, pp 8-11; accessed Jan 2017 < http://digitalcommons.olivet.edu/cgi/viewcontent.cgi?article=1524&context=cotn_pm >

7. Herbert McGonigle, "John Henry Jowett: The Man, His Message, and His Method [If we study the giants we are less likely to be pygmies]", *Preacher's Magazine*, Vol. 46, No. 6, June 1971, pp 9-11 & 45; accessed March 2015 at < http://digitalcommons.olivet.edu/cgi/viewcontent.cgi?article=1527&context=cotn_pm>

8. Herbert McGonigle, "Architects of Wesleyan Theology, I: John Fletcher", *Nazarene Preacher*, Vol. 47, No. 3, March 1972, pp 14-16 & 45-46; accessed Feb 2016 at < http://digitalcommons.olivet.edu/cgi/viewcontent.cgi?article=1536&context=cotn_pm >

9. Herbert McGonigle, "Architects of Wesleyan Theology, Part II: Adam Clarke", *Nazarene Preacher*, Vol. 47, No. 4, April 1972, pp 14-16 & 41-43; accessed Feb 2016 at < http://digitalcommons.olivet.edu/cgi/viewcontent.cgi?article=1537&context=cotn_pm >

10. Herbert McGonigle, "Architects of Wesleyan Theology, No. III: Richard Watson", *Nazarene Preacher*, Vol. 47, No. 5, May 1972, pp 35-38, accessed Jan 2016 at < http://digitalcommons.olivet.edu/cgi/viewcontent.cgi?article=1538&context=cotn_pm >

11. Herbert McGonigle, "Architects of Wesleyan Theology, IV: W. B. Pope", *Preacher's Magazine*, Vol. 47, No. 6, June 1972, pp 9-12; accessed Feb 2016 at < http://digitalcommons.olivet.edu/cgi/viewcontent.cgi?article=1539&context=cotn_pm >

12. Herbert McGonigle, "The Father of the English Bible" [Little is known of William Tyndale's early life, but more than any other one man he deserves the title Father of the English Bible], *Preacher's Magazine*, Vol. 48, No. 3, March 1973, pp 15-16 & 17-18; accessed Feb 2016 at <

http://digitalcommons.olivet.edu/cgi/viewcontent.cgi?article=1548&context=cotn_pm >

13. Herbert McGonigle, "Pneumatological Nomenclature in Early Methodism", *Wesleyan Theological Journal*, Vol.8, Spring 1973, pp 61-72.

14. Herbert McGonigle, "The Pastor as Preacher", *Preacher's Magazine*, Vol. 50, No. 8, August 1975, pp 3-6; accessed Feb 2016 at < http://digitalcommons.olivet.edu/cgi/viewcontent.cgi?article=1577&context=cotn_pm>

15. Herbert McGonigle, "William Cooke – A Model for Holiness Preachers" [The "Lion of Lincolnshire" made his mark as a Wesleyan teacher, theologian, and preacher of the Word], *Preacher's Magazine*, Vol. 51, No. 12, December 1976, pp 3-5; < http://digitalcommons.olivet.edu/cgi/viewcontent.cgi?article=1593&context=cotn_pm>

16. Herbert McGonigle (ed.). *William Cooke on Entire Sanctification*. Kansas City, Missouri: Beacon Hill Press, 1978.

17. Herbert McGonigle, "Wesley's Revision of the Shorter Catechism", *Preacher's Magazine*, Vol. 56, No. 1, September, October, November, 1980, pp 59 & 62-63; accessed Feb 2016 at < http://digitalcommons.olivet.edu/cgi/viewcontent.cgi?article=1618&context=cotn_pm>

18. Herbert McGonigle, contributed six entries to *Beacon Dictionary of Theology*, ed., Richard S. Taylor; Kansas City: Beacon Hill Press of Kansas City, 1983; namely: "Anglo-Israelism"; "Divine Decrees"; "Fall, The"; "Liturgy, Liturgics"; "Remnant"; and "Zionism" [these articles also accessed online, 2 May 2017, at < http://ininet.org/theology-beacon-dictionary-of-theology.html >

19. Herbert McGonigle, "Church Planting: New Testament Style", *Preacher's Magazine*, Vol. 58, No. 3, March/April/May 1983, pp 30-31 accessed March 2016 at < http://digitalcommons.olivet.edu/cgi/viewcontent.cgi?article=1628&context=cotn_pm>

20. Herbert McGonigle, "Adam Clarke: Holiness Saint and Scholar", *Preacher's Magazine*, Vol. 59, No.1, Sep. Oct. Nov., 1983; accessed on 20 June 2014 at < http://www.usacanadaregion.org/sites/usacanadaregion.org/files/Roots/Resources/Adam-Clarke-Holiness-Saint-and-Scholar.pdf>

21. Herbert McGonigle, "Holiness Preaching Today", *Preacher's Magazine*, June, July, August 1985, pp 51- 53; accessed March 2014 at <

http://digitalcommons.olivet.edu/cgi/viewcontent.cgi?article=1637&conte xt=cotn_pm>

22. Herbert McGonigle. "John Fletcher's Influence on Wesleyan Theology", *The Flame*, July/August 1985, Vol. 51, No. 4, pp 3-5.

23. Herbert McGonigle. *Dr Adam Clarke's Understanding of Christian Holiness* (A paper read at a meeting of the Wesley Fellowship at Zion Church, Handsworth, Birmingham on 11 October 1986) [Privately photocopied and distributed, Birmingham: The Wesley Fellowship, 1986].

24. Herbert McGonigle. *John Fletcher's 'Checks to Antinomianism' – An Evaluation.* A Paper read at a meeting of the Wesley Fellowship at Stoke-on-Trent on Saturday, 3rd October 1987. [Biddulph, Staffordshire: Wesley Fellowship, 1987].

25. Herbert McGonigle, "Significant Wesleyan Milestones: 1738, 1788, 1988", *Preacher's Magazine*, Vol. 63, No. 3, March, April, May 1988, pp 32ff; accessed March 2015 at < http://digitalcommons.olivet.edu/cgi/viewcontent.cgi?article=1648&conte xt=cotn_pm>

26. Herbert McGonigle. *The Arminianism of John Wesley*. Occasional Paper No. 3 of the Wesley Fellowship. Ilkeston: The Wesley Fellowship, 1988.

27. Herbert McGonigle. "Question from a Cambridge member", *Newsletter of the Wesley Fellowship*, July 1992, p. 1. [Question: Did John Wesley believe babies are born 'in depravity' because Adam's sin was transmitted to all succeeding generations?"]

28. Herbert McGonigle. *John Wesley and the Moravians*. Wesley Fellowship Occasional Paper No. 8. Ilkeston: Published on behalf of the Wesley Fellowship by Moorleys Print & Publishing, 1993.

29. Herbert McGonigle. "Questions and Answers", *Wesley Fellowship Quarterly*, May 1993, p. 1. [Question: "Did John Wesley say something about wanting one-hundred men on fire for God who would bring revival?"]

30. Herbert McGonigle. "Questions and Answers", *Wesley Fellowship Quarterly*, May 1994 (*sic.*), p. 1. (Note this *Quarterly* issue was issued incorrectly dated "May, 1944"). [Question: "Which book on John Wesley would you recommend to someone studying him for the first time?"]

31. Herbert Boyd McGonigle, "John Wesley: Evangelical Arminian" (unpublished PhD diss. University of Keele, 2 vols, 1994). [Subsequently revised and published as Sufficient Saving Grace: John Wesley's Evangelical Arminianism, 2001; see below]

32. Herbert McGonigle, *John Wesley's Doctrine of Prevenient Grace*. Ilkeston: The Wesley Fellowship in collaboration with Moorleys Print & Publishing, 1995a.

33. Herbert McGonigle. *Scriptural Holiness: The Wesleyan Distinctive*. The 1995 Maynard James Memorial Lecture. Ilkeston: The Flame Trust, 1995b.

34. Herbert McGonigle. "Question Box". *Wesley Fellowship Quarterly*, April 1995, p. 1. [This is an example of a regular column where Dr McGonigle invites his readers (of Wesley Fellowship newsletters – also similarly in *The Flame*) to send in "queries about Wesley dates, quotations, history, theology, etc." which he will endeavour to answer succinctly and plainly. The questions here deal with recommendations of "Wesleyan devotional notes" and "textbooks of systematic Wesleyan theology".]

35. Herbert McGonigle. "Questions and Answers", *Wesley Fellowship Quarterly*, July 1995, p. 1. [Question: "Did John Wesley write a commentary on the whole Bible?"]

36. Herbert McGonigle. "Wesleyan Arminianism", Page 5 in *Wesley Pieces: Conference and Other Papers 1995*. Edited by Paul Taylor. Lutterworth: The Wesley Fellowship, 1996.

37. Herbert McGonigle. "Questions and Answers", *Wesley Fellowship Quarterly*, February 1997, p. 1. [Question: "I heard a preacher say that John Wesley wrote that there was not one day of his past life that he would want to relive. Can you tell me if Wesley did say that?"]

38. Herbert McGonigle. "John Wesley's Eschatology', pp. 153-175 in *Windows on Wesley: Wesleyan Theology in Today's World*, ed. Philip R. Meadows. Oxford: Applied Theology Press, 1997.

39. Herbert McGonigle. "Questions and Answers", *Wesley Fellowship Quarterly*, November 1997, p. 1. [Question: "Recently I heard a speaker say that John Wesley once said that there is no spirituality but what is social. Did he say that, and, if so, what did it mean?]

40. Herbert McGonigle. "Questions and Answers", *Wesley Fellowship Quarterly*, September 1999, p. 1. [Question: "Did John Wesley ever participate in anything that might be called the charisma of tongues?"]

41. Herbert McGonigle, contributed 23 entries to *A Dictionary of Methodism in Britain and Ireland*, ed., John A Vickers; Peterborough: Epworth Press, 2000; namely: "Church of the Nazarene (UK)"; "Cownley, Joseph"; "Haime, John"; "Hanby, Thomas"; "Holiness"; "Holiness Movement"; "Hopper, Christopher"; "Hunter, William"; "Inwood, Dr Charles"; "Jaco, Peter"; "Love-feast"; "Maxfield, Thomas"; "Mitchell, Thomas"; "Murlin, John"; "Olivers, Thomas"; "Pietism"; "Rankin, Thomas"; "Staniforth,

Sampson"; "Story, George"; "Valton, John"; "Walsh, Thomas"; "Whitefield, George"; and "Wright, Duncan"; articles accessible online, on 20 April 2017, at < http://www.wesleyhistoricalsociety.org.uk/dmbi/index.php >

42. Herbert McGonigle. "Your Questions Answered", *Wesley Fellowship Quarterly*, May 2000, p. 2. [Question: "Did John Wesley ever speak of entire sanctification as the eradication of original sin?"]

43. Herbert McGonigle. "Questions and Answers", *Wesley Fellowship Quarterly*, September 2000, pp. 2-3. [Question: "Was Charles Wesley an open-air preacher like his brother John and is there any record of his ministry?"]

44. Herbert McGonigle. "Your Questions Answered", *Wesley Fellowship Quarterly*, December 2000, pp. 3-4. [Question 1: "The first has to do with a statement that 'without grace man is like the beasts of the field'". Question 2: "Did Wesley actually say, 'The world is my parish'"? Question 3: "Is it true that John Wesley thought that the souls of the departed saved are in paradise and 'preparing' for heaven?"]

45. Herbert Boyd McGonigle. *Sufficient Saving Grace: John Wesley's Evangelical Arminianism*. Carlisle: Paternoster Press, 2001.

46. Herbert McGonigle. "Your Questions Answered", *Wesley Fellowship Quarterly*, April 2001, pp. 2-3. [Question: "Did [John Wesley] ever say or write the words: 'Do all the good you can, By all the means you can, In all the ways you can, In all the places you can, At all the times you can, To all the people you can, As long as ever you can?'"]

47. Herbert McGonigle. "A Tribute to the late Revd Dr William Parkes", *Wesley Fellowship Quarterly*, October 2001, pp. 1-4. [The Revd Dr William Parkes (1933-2001) was co-founder of the Wesley Fellowship with Herbert McGonigle in 1985.]

48. Herbert McGonigle. "Your Questions Answered", *Wesley Fellowship Quarterly*, May 2002, pp. 3-4. [Question: "Is it true that Samuel Wesley junior was strongly opposed to the preaching of his brothers John and Charles and thought it was madness?"]

49. Herbert McGonigle, *To God be the Glory: A Short History of the Killadeas Camp Meeting Convention to Celebrate its Golden Jubilee, 1952-2002*, Killadeas [Co. Fermanagh, Northern Ireland]: Killadeas Convention Committee, July 2002.

50. Herbert McGonigle, "John Wesley – Exemplar of the Catholic Spirit". Pages 50-68 in *Ecumenism and History: Studies in Honour of John H. Y. Briggs*. Edited by Anthony R. Cross. Carlisle: Paternoster Press, 2002.

51. Herbert McGonigle. "Your Questions Answered", *Wesley Fellowship Quarterly*, February 2003, pp. 2-3. [Question: "One of our WF members has asked about the claims made that John Wesley's preaching often produced hysterical reactions among his hearers and that Wesley encouraged these responses."]

52. Herbert Boyd McGonigle. *Sufficient Saving Grace: John Wesley's Evangelical Arminianism*. [Reprinted with corrections especially regarding the index]. Carlisle: Paternoster Press, 2003.

53. Herbert McGonigle. "Your Questions Answered", *Wesley Fellowship Quarterly*, September 2003, p. 2. [Question: "I read in an anthology of quotations that John Wesley said that he burned all his sermons every seven years, because he felt he should be able to compose better sermons than he had done earlier. Is this true?"]

54. Herbert McGonigle. "Your Questions Answered", *Wesley Fellowship Quarterly*, December 2003, pp 3-4. [Question 1: "Did John Wesley say something about revival being linked to the doctrine of Christian perfection?"; Question 2: "Did John Wesley say that the 18th Century revival would embrace the whole world?"; Question 3: "Did John Wesley say that God always works in answer to prayer?"]

55. Herbert McGonigle. "Your Questions Answered", *Wesley Fellowship Quarterly*, March 2004, pp. 3-4. [Question 1: "Is it true that John Wesley wrote a dictionary?"; Question 2: "Where can I find the statement by John Wesley that the whole world was his parish?"; Question 3: "Is it true that John Wesley and George Whitefield quarrelled over the doctrine of predestination?"]

56. Herbert McGonigle. ". . . Reviews of [selected] Wesley Fellowship Publications", *Wesley Fellowship Quarterly*, July 2004, pp. 5-8. [The books reviewed include those by: Paul Taylor & Howard Mellor (*Travelling Man*, 1994); John Lawson (*Conversion of the Wesleys: 1738 Reconsidered*, 1987); William M. Greathouse (*John Wesley's Theology of Christian Perfection*, 1989); Oliver A. Beckerlegge (*Charles Wesley: Poet*, 1990); Sydney Martin (*John Wesley and the Witness of the Spirit*, 1990); Barry Bryant (*John Wesley on the Origins of Evil*, 1992); & Edward Houghton (*Handmaid of Piety*, 1992).]

57. Herbert McGonigle, "William Bramwell: A Re-Appraisal" [The Wesley Historical Society 2004 Annual Lecture, presented during the Methodist Conference at Loughborough, Monday 28 June 2004], in *Proceedings of the Wesley Historical Society* Vol. 54, No. 6 (Oct. 2004): 219-236.

58. Herbert McGonigle. *John Wesley's Arminian Theology: An Introduction.* Second Edition of the 1988 Wesley Fellowship Occasional Paper No. 3. Revised and reset. Shearsby: The Wesley Fellowship, 2005.

59. Herbert McGonigle. "Your Questions Answered", *Wesley Fellowship Quarterly*, April 2005, pp. 3-4. [Question: "John Wesley's 'Puritan ancestors.' What does this mean? I always thought his ancestors were Anglicans."]

60. Herbert McGonigle. "Your Questions Answered", *Wesley Fellowship Quarterly*, July 2005, pp. 2-3. [Two questions – and answers – dealing with quotations attributed to John Wesley]

61. Herbert Boyd McGonigle. Foreword to *The Ground of Election: Jacobus Arminius' Doctrine of the Work and Person of Christ*, by F. Stuart Clarke. Bletchley, Milton Keynes: Paternoster, 2006.

62. Herbert McGonigle. "Your Questions Answered", *Wesley Fellowship Bulletin*, Spring 2006, p. 3. [Question: "Is it true that John Wesley didn't like Quakers?"]

63. Herbert McGonigle. "Your Questions Answered", *Wesley Fellowship Bulletin*, Autumn 2006, pp. 2-3. [Question: "Did John Wesley really translate the Bible into English?"]

64. Herbert B McGonigle, "Celebrating Two Centuries of Freedom: 1807-2007", in: *Decision* [Magazine of the Billy Graham Evangelistic Association], January/February 2007, pp 9-12.

65. Herbert McGonigle. "Your Questions Answered", *Wesley Fellowship Bulletin*, Spring 2007, pp. 2-3. [Question: "The quotation 'Cleanliness is next to godliness' is attributed to John Wesley. Did he say that and could you please tell me where I can find it?"]

66. Herbert B McGonigle. Foreword to *A Thousand Tongues: The Wesley hymns as a guide to scriptural teaching* by John Lawson, Paternoster Press: London, 2007, pp 8-10.

67. Herbert McGonigle. "Your Questions Answered", *Wesley Fellowship Bulletin*, Autumn 2007, pp. 2-3. [Question: "Did John Wesley say somewhere in his writings that he was a Roman Catholic?"]

68. Herbert McGonigle. "Your Questions Answered", *Wesley Fellowship Bulletin*, Spring 2008, pp. 2-4. [Question 1: Please can you help me with a John Wesley quotation . . . saying that a hundred preachers would soon bring revival. Did he actually say that?"; Question 2: "Recently I saw a hymn, said to have been written by John Wesley, which spoke about the

Jews returning to Israel and becoming Christians. Do you know anything about this hymn?"]

69. Herbert McGonigle. "Your Questions Answered", *Wesley Fellowship Bulletin*, Autumn 2008, pp. 2-3. [Question: "I've seen a picture of John Wesley standing and preaching on his father's grave. Did this just happen once or many times?"].

70. Herbert B. McGonigle. Foreword to *Wesley as a Pastoral Theologian: Theological Methodology in John Wesley's Doctrine of Christian Perfection*, by David B. McEwan. Milton Keynes: Paternoster, 2009.

71. Herbert McGonigle, "The Four Alls of Methodism – 4/4", From Methodist Evangelicals Together website, < http://www.met-uk.org/met/events.php>, accessed 20 Sept, 2010.

72. Herbert Boyd McGonigle. *A Burning and a Shining Light: The Life and Ministry of William Bramwell*. Sheffield: The Wesley Fellowship, in association with Moorleys Print & Publishing, 2009.

73. Herbert Boyd McGonigle. *Christianity or Deism? John Wesley's Response to John Taylor's Denial of the Doctrine of Original Sin*, Sheffield: The Wesley Fellowship, 2012. [A version of this paper was first read by Dr McGonigle at a meeting of the Tyndale Fellowship at Cambridge, UK, in 2005; this version was edited for publication on behalf of The Wesley Fellowship by William T. Graham].

74. *Herbert McGonigle, *John Wesley: Exemplar of the Catholic Spirit*, Ilkeston: Commissioned with Moorleys Print & Publishing, 2014a. [Reprint of an essay (cited above) first published in *Ecumenism and History: Studies in Honour of John H. Y. Briggs*, ed. Anthony R. Cross, published by Paternoster Press, 2002].

75. *Herbert McGonigle, *Charles Wesley: For All, For All, My Saviour Died*, Ilkeston: Commissioned with Moorleys Print & Publishing, 2014b.

76. *Herbert McGonigle, *John Wesley: The Death of Christ*, Ilkeston: Commissioned with Moorleys Print & Publishing, 2014c.

77. *Herbert Boyd McGonigle, *Epworth: The Cradle of Methodism*, Ilkeston: Commissioned with Moorleys Print & Publishing, 2014d.

78. *Herbert Boyd McGonigle, *John Wesley: Doctrine of Final Judgement*, Ilkeston: Commissioned with Moorleys Print & Publishing, 2015a.

79. *Herbert McGonigle, *Thomas Walsh: Saint and Scholar*, Ilkeston: Commissioned with Moorleys Print & Publishing, 2015b.

80. *Herbert McGonigle, *Our Story: Autobiographical thoughts from the pen of Revd Dr Herbert B McGonigle*, Manchester: Nazarene Theological College Archives, 2015c.

81. *Herbert Boyd McGonigle, *Dr Adam Clarke: Methodist Preacher and Scholar*, Ilkeston: Commissioned with Moorleys Print & Publishing, 2015d.

82. *Herbert Boyd McGonigle, *Gideon Ouseley: Methodist Preacher and Biblical Scholar*, Ilkeston: Commissioned with Moorleys Print & Publishing, 2015e.

83. *Herbert Boyd McGonigle, *Thomas Cook: Evangelist and Saint*, Ilkeston: Commissioned with Moorleys Print & Publishing, 2016a.

84. *Herbert Boyd McGonigle, *The Methodist Pentecost, 1758-1763*, Ilkeston: Commissioned with Moorleys Print & Publishing, 2016b.

85. *Herbert Boyd McGonigle, *John Fletcher: Methodist Saint and Scholar*, Ilkeston: Commissioned with Moorleys Print & Publishing, 2016c.

86. *Herbert Boyd McGonigle, *An Appreciation of Revd Dr John Henry Jowett's "Heaven's Hallelujah*", Ilkeston: Commissioned with Moorleys Print & Publishing, 2016c.

87. *Herbert Boyd McGonigle, *General William Booth*, Ilkeston: Commissioned with Moorleys Print & Publishing, 2016d.

88. *Herbert Boyd McGonigle, *John Wesley on The Great Salvation*, Ilkeston: Commissioned with Moorleys Print & Publishing, 2017a. [Note: This publication contains (in pp 1-26) a significant chapter entitled 'John Wesley: The Supremacy of Grace', which was apparently written before 2009 and has, it seems, not been published hitherto].

89. *Herbert Boyd McGonigle, *Samuel Chadwick: Preacher and Evangelist*, Ilkeston: Commissioned with Moorleys Print & Publishing, 2017b.

90. *Herbert Boyd McGonigle, *Francis William Crossley*, Ilkeston: Commissioned with Moorleys Print & Publishing, 2018a.

91. *Herbert Boyd McGonigle, *Dr Alexander Maclaren: Preacher and Expositer*, Ilkeston: Commissioned with Moorleys Print & Publishing, 2018a.

92. *Herbert Boyd McGonigle, *Herbert and Jeanne McGonigle: Our Story*, Ilkeston: Commissioned with Moorleys Print & Publishing, 2018b.

93. *Herbert Boyd McGonigle, *Through the Year with John and Charles Wesley*, Ilkeston: Commissioned with Moorleys Print & Publishing, 2019.

94. [Projected for 2020] Herbert Boyd McGonigle, *To Know One Thing: John Wesley, The Didsbury Lectures, 2002.*

....

SELECTED ARTICLES WRITTEN BY HERBERT MCGONIGLE PUBLISHED IN THE *THE FLAME* FROM 1963 TO 2014 (AS LISTED BY HIM IN 2014), INCLUDE:

1. "Hanged Upon a Comma!", Jan-Feb 1963 [his first article published in the magazine].
2. "The Mormon Menace".
3. "September Glory in Manchester".
4. "Extracts from the Writings of Mrs Mary Fletcher".
5. "I Believe in the Holy Ghost".
6. "Bombshell on the Theologian Playground".
7. "Dr Lockyer: Sanctification and Security".
8. "The Man of Romans Seven: Saint or Sinner?"
9. "The Man of Romans Seven: Why the Present Tense?"
10. "In the Steps of John Wesley".
11. "The Burning Heart".
12. "The Apostle of the Haphazard".
13. "Adventure in Evangelism".
14. "What Holiness Means to Me".
15. "How F.B. Meyer Received The Holy Spirit".
16. "Elect in the Sun".
17. "I Have Received an Extraordinary Baptism of the Spirit".
18. "The Gospel of Power".
19. "Commissioner Brengle and the Gifts of the Spirit".
20. "Books Received".
21. "He Followed in Wesley's Steps: The Ministry of Charles Inwood".
22. "The Methodist Pentecost".
23. "The Tragedy and Triumph of Masada".
24. "The Incarnation: Fact or Fiction".
25. "Pentecostal Doctrine".
26. "A Personal Plea from the Associate Editor".
27. "The Editorial Board".
28. "Dr William Cooke on Entire Sanctification".

29. "The Baptism with the Holy Spirit: What is It?"
30. "The Second Coming of Christ".
31. "A Bible Commentary for Today".
32. "Personal Impressions of the USA".
33. "*The Flame*: 46 Years of Proclaiming Full Salvation".
34. "Calvinism and English Calvinism – A Theological Bombshell".
35. "Book Reviews".
36. "Why I Believe in the Virgin Birth".
37. "Gospel Gleanings from the Greek".
38. "A Challenge to all our Reporters".
39. "The Pope's Visit to Britain".
40. "What do we mean by Holiness Preaching?"
41. "A Good Half-Guinea's Worth".
42. "Baptised by Fire".
43. "Salute to Martin Luther".
44. "Give Attention to Reading".
45. "Singing with the Understanding".
46. "Fifty Years of Full Salvation Witness".
47. "John Fletcher's Influence on Wesley's Theology".
48. "Introducing the Wesley Fellowship".
49. "Gospel Gleanings from the Greek New Testament".
50. "The Inextinguishable Blaze".
51. "That Man of God – Peter Bohler".
52. "Killedeas Camp-Meeting".
53. "My Chains fell off".
54. "Calling Sinners to Repentance".
55. "To All Our Readers".
56. "A Great Man and a Prince is Fallen in Israel".
57. "Compelling Poor Sinners to Come In".
58. "I Believe in St Patrick".
59. "Apostle of England: John Wesley".
60. "Preaching in Gwennap Pit: John Wesley's Cornish Pulpit".
61. "He Breaks the Power of Cancelled Sin".
62. "The Revd Dr Arthur Skevington Wood: 1916-1993".
63. "John Calvin, John Wesley and Predestination".
64. "Nazarene Leadership Speaks Out on Homosexuality".
65. "Father of the English Bible".
66. "*The Flame*: Personal Reflections".

67. "A Tribute to Leonard Ravenhill".
68. "John Wesley and the Toronto Experience: Are they Linked?"
69. "Scriptural Holiness in a Post-Christian Britain".
70. "Trewint – Where Time Stands Still".
71. "A Manifesto for Revival".
72. "Salvation Story".
73. "Songs of Victory".
74. "The Anointing: Yesterday, Today and Forever".
75. "Travel: Impressions of Japan".
76. "Re-minting Christian Holiness".
77. "Every Preacher Should Read This".
78. "A Brand from the Burning: The Life of John Wesley".
79. "Nothing to do But Save Souls".
80. "Mary, Mary, Quite Contrary?"
81. "Tribute to the Revd Maurice Winterburn, 1914-2005".
82. "Wesley's Ways and Wesley's Days".
83. Wesley's Ways and Wesley's Days: Man of One Book".
84. "We are all Charismatic: Bible Speaks".
85. "Wesley's Ways and Wesley's Days: John Wesley and the Methodist Pentecost".
86. "John Henry Jowett" (Two *Flames*).
87. "Kindled by a Spark of Grace: Re-calling Revival in Leeds".
88. "A Burning and Shining Light: William Bramwell".
89. "A Thousand Tongues".
90. "The Devil Hates Field Preaching!"
91. "Peter Gentry".
92. "The Religion of the Heart: John Wesley's Religion".
93. "Charles Wesley: Orpheus of the Christian Church".
94. "John Wesley's Doctrine of Eternal Punishment" (Two *Flames*).
95. "Glory to God in the High Street!"
96. "When Life Tumbles In – What Then?"
97. "Abide with Me: Henry Francis Lyte".

....

Selected Articles (29) written by Herbert McGonigle for the 'Children's Page' in *The Flame* (as listed by him in 2014)

***The Flame*: 1963**:
"Adam Clarke"; "The Gipsy Bible Seller"; "Gospel Bells"; "Telling the Good News"; "The Day of Small Things"; "How *Ben Hur* was Written".
***The Flame*: 1964**:
"Friend of the Redskins"; "Treasures in a Book"; "Cheerio!"; "Greyfriars' Bobby"; "The Hill of Blood"; "Do we need a Bible Museum?".
***The Flame* 1965**:
"Saint Nicholas"; "How the Burglar was Converted"; "The Friendship of Damon and Phintias"; "Mickey and the Door of the Heart"; "How King Richard Escaped"; "The Miner's Son".
***The Flame*: 1966**:
"The Princess and the Old Umbrella"; "The King Musician"; "Iron Gates"; "The Worst Place on Earth"; "Keep the Lamps Alight!"; "The Living Submarine!".
***The Flame*: 1967**:
"The Sweet Singer of Wales"; "A Famous German Artist"; "The Romance of Writing"; "The One who Ran Away"; "Among the Eskimos".

....

Selected Recordings of Revd Dr Herbert McGonigle preaching or Lecturing

Didsbury Lectures, 2002: 'To Know One Thing'
Published as a set of four CDs by Nazarene Theological College, Dene Road, Didsbury, Manchester, UK, details available from the Archivist at archives@nazarene.ac.uk
Herbert B McGonigle, "John Wesley and Scripture", Lecture One, published as CD: 01;
Herbert McGonigle, "John Wesley and Prevenient Grace", Lecture Two, published as CD: 02;
Herbert McGonigle, "John Wesley and Salvation", Lecture Three, published as CD: 03;
Herbert McGonigle, "John Wesley and Evangelism", Lecture Four, published as CD: 04.

....

Asbury Theological Seminary Chapel Services Recordings

01. Herbert McGonigle, "John Wesley's Defense of the Doctrine of Original Sin", 28 Feb 2006. Chapel Services Recording made by Asbury Theological

Seminary, Wilmore, Kentucky, USA, published 2011 as an mp3 at < https://place.asburyseminary.edu/ecommonsatschapelservices/1053/>

02. Herbert Boyd McGonigle, "Knowing Christ", Jan. 2006. Chapel Services Recording made by Asbury Theological Seminary, Wilmore, Kentucky, USA, published 2006, available as an mp3 at < https://place.asburyseminary.edu/ecommonsatschapelservices/5030/ >
03. Herbert McGonigle, "Nothing to do but save souls: John Wesley and evangelism", February, 27, 2006, Chapel Services Recording made by Asbury Theological Seminary, Wilmore, Kentucky, USA, published 2011, available as an mp3 recording available at < https://place.asburyseminary.edu/ecommonsatschapelservices/4305/ >

....

SELECTED BIOGRAPHICAL ARTICLES PUBLISHED IN VARIOUS PUBLICATIONS ABOUT THE LIFE AND WORK OF THE REV DR HERBERT MCGONIGLE INCLUDE:

1. [William T. Graham], "Dr Herbert McGonigle retires as College Principal to take up a new post", in: *The Flame*, Vol. 70, No. 4, October-December 2004, 5-6. [See also the addendum "Note" published in *The Flame*, Vol. 71, No. 1, January-March 2005, p. 20].
2. Joseph W. Cunningham and David Rainey, eds., *The Path of Holiness: Perspectives in Wesleyan Thought in Honour of Herbert B. McGonigle*, Lexington, Kentucky: Emeth Press, 2014.
3. Various issues of *Together*, [a magazine currently published by the British Isles North District & British Isles South District Church of the Nazarene, general editor Rev Colin H Wood, Glasgow]; for example a short eulogy on the late Mrs Jeanne McGonigle is published under the heading: 'In Memoriam', *Together*, No. 28, Spring 2017, p. 2, accessible online at < https://www.nazarene.org.uk/index.php/2-uncategorised/12-together-magazine >
4. Since Dr McGonigle's retirement, following a serious stroke in 2009, he has not stopped writing! He has embarked on privately publishing a series of attractively produced little books (marked in this present bibliography with an asterisk *), in which he has thoughtfully invited various colleagues and friends to write a foreword. Accordingly, each of these forewords provide a range of biographical insights into the life and ministry of Dr

McGonigle and his gifted wife Jeanne (who wonderfully supported his work for more than fifty-five years before she went to be with her Lord on 5 February 2017, aged nearly 96 years). A good example of this is the foreword to Dr McGonigle's book: *John Wesley on The Great Salvation*, Ilkeston: Commissioned with Moorleys Print & Publishing, 2017. In it, the Rev Karl Stanfield (who, in the early 1980s was an undergraduate student in Dr McGonigle's classes in Homiletics, Church History and Wesley Studies at the Nazarene College in Didsbury, Manchester, and who since 1990 has been Pastor of the Nazarene church that Dr McGonigle attends in Brooklands, Manchester) recounts times, stretching from 1981 to 2017, when he has appreciated knowing Herbert and Jeanne McGonigle.

....

Publications associated directly or indirectly with the Wesley Fellowship (arranged in approximate order of date of publication) include the following items (revised 09 December 2017, by W T Graham):

From its beginning in 1985, the Wesley Fellowship was active in promoting the serious study of Wesleyan history, theology and experience. John and Charles Wesley were prodigious publishers of Christian literature in their own time. With their own original writings and their many extracted and edited works, they published more than four hundred separate titles. These were made up of sermons, letters, hymns, journals, Biblical commentaries, theological treatises, including the 50-volume set of A *Christian Library*. The Wesley Fellowship could never compare its published outflow with that of the Wesley brothers! Nevertheless, it disseminated numerous *Newsletters*, *Occasional Papers*[20] and more substantial works for more than a quarter of a century from 1985. What follows is a provisional list, in approximate date order of publication, of the Fellowship's more important publications and other associated items.

1. *A. Skevington Wood. *Love Excluding Sin: Wesley's doctrine of Sanctification.* Occasional Paper No. 1. Biddulph: The Wesley Fellowship, 1986.

2. Lionel Clement M. Hawker. *Wesley's Doctrine of Prevenient Grace.* Didsbury: The Wesley Fellowship, 1986.

---

[20] Wesley Fellowship "Occasional Papers" are marked by an asterisk (*) in this document.

3. Harold E. Moore. *Let the Earth Hear His Voice: The Devotional Use of Charles Wesley's Hymns*. [A synopsis of a Paper read to a meeting of the Wesley Fellowship at British Isles Nazarene College, Didsbury 7 March 1986.] [Manchester: The Wesley Fellowship, 1986].

4. Barry E. Bryant. *The Wesleys' and Holy Communion: New Wine into Old Wineskins*. A paper read at a meeting of The Wesley Fellowship at Zion Church, Handsworth, Birmingham on Saturday 11 October 1986. [Manchester: The Wesley Fellowship, 1986]

5. Herbert McGonigle. *Dr. Adam Clarke's Understanding of Christian Holiness*. A paper read at the meeting of the Wesley Fellowship at Zion Church, Handsworth, Birmingham, on Saturday, 11 October 1986. [Manchester: The Wesley Fellowship, 1986]

6. William Parkes. *The Love Feast: Primitive Christian Practice in a Wesleyan Setting*. Birmingham: The Wesley Fellowship, 1986.

7. Herbert McGonigle. *John Fletcher's 'Checks to Antinomianism' – An Evaluation*. Stoke on Trent: The Wesley Fellowship, 1987.

8. E. Dorothy Graham. *Female Primitive Methodist Travelling Preachers*. Stoke-on-Trent: The Wesley Fellowship, 1987.

9. *John Lawson. *The Conversion of the Wesleys: 1738 Reconsidered*. [Occasional Paper No. 2.] Ilkeston: Moorleys Print & Publishing, 1987, pp.37.

10. *Herbert McGonigle. *The Arminianism of John Wesley*. Occasional Paper No. 3 of the Wesley Fellowship. Ilkeston: Moorleys Print & Publishing, 1988. pp.36.

11. *William M. Greathouse. *John Wesley's Theology of Christian Perfection*. [Occasional Paper No. 4.] Ilkeston: Moorleys, Print & Publishing, 1989.

12. *Sydney Martin. John *Wesley and The Witness of the Spirit*. [Occasional Paper No. 5.] Ilkeston: Moorleys Print & Publishing, 1990. pp.37.

13. *Oliver A. Beckerlegge. *Charles Wesley: Poet*. [Occasional Paper No. 6.] Ilkeston: Moorleys Print & Publishing, 1990. pp.29.

14. William T Graham. *Wesley's Early Experiments in Education: with special reference to girls at Kingswood School*. Ilkeston: Moorleys Print & Publishing, 1990.

15. John S. Isherwood. *John Wesley: Evangelist* [An address given to the Wesley Fellowship at Zion Holiness Church, Birmingham on 2nd March 1991]. [Birkenhead]: Emmanuel Bible College, 1991.

16. Allan Longworth. *A Brother Bereft: A Study of Samuel Wesley in relation to his Brother John*. Ilkeston: Moorleys Print & Publishing, n.d. [c.1991]

17. Arthur Skevington Wood. *Third Wave or Second Coming? The Relevance of Biblical Prophecy*. The 1991 Maynard James Memorial Lecture. Ilkeston: The Flame Trust in association with Moorleys Print & Publishing, 1992.

18. Barry E. Bryant. 'Wesley's "Christian System" and His Doctrine of Sin'. An address to the Faculty of Nazarene Theological College, Manchester, 13 May 1992. [Manchester: unpublished paper, photocopied and privately distributed, 1992].

19. *Barry Bryant. *John Wesley on the Origins of Evil*. [Occasional Paper No. 7.] Moorleys Print & Publishing, Ilkeston. 1992. pp.26.

20. Edward Houghton. *Handmaid of Piety and other papers on Charles Wesley's Hymns*. Quacks Books, York, in Association with the Wesley Fellowship. 1992. pp.125.

21. Arthur Skevington Wood. *Revelation and Reason: Wesleyan Responses to Eighteenth-Century Rationalism*. The Wesley Fellowship, Bulkington, Nuneaton, 1992. ISBN 0951633228. pp.103.

22. Charles H. Goodwin. *A Dismal Notoriety: The Rise and Progress of Methodism at Wednesbury between 1742-1744 in the light of New England Revivalism*. Cannock: Charles H. Goodwin, 1993.

23. *Herbert McGonigle. *John Wesley and the Moravians*. [Occasional Paper, No. 8.] The Wesley Fellowship in association with Moorleys Print & Publishing, Ilkeston, 1993. pp.32. ISBN 0 86071 422 5.

24. Paul Taylor & Howard Mellor, eds. *Travelling Man: A Tribute to the Life and Ministry of the Reverend Dr Arthur Skevington Wood.*, Ilkeston: Moorleys Print & Publishing, 1994. ISBN 1 898362 05 X. p/b. pp.126.

25. John Isherwood. *William Seward and the Wesleys.* Lecture at a meeting of the Wesley Fellowship, in Birmingham on 16 April 1994. Birkenhead: Emmanuel Bible College, 1994. (Note: although not technically a Wesley Fellowship document, John Isherwood, shortly before he died, published privately in 2014 a supplement to this paper, entitled: *The Story of William Seward (1702-1740): From stockbroker to field-preacher*. Bodmin: Printbridge (16 Castle Street, Bodmin, Cornwall, PL31 2DU), [2014].)

26. William Parkes. *The Arminian Methodists. The Derby Faith: A Wesleyan Aberration in Pursuit of Revivalism and Holiness*. Merlin Monograph, Cannock, Staffordshire, 1995, reprinted and published by The Wesley Fellowship, [1995]. pp.53.

27. *Herbert McGonigle. *John Wesley's Doctrine of Prevenient Grace.* [Occasional Paper No. 9.] Moorleys Print & Publishing in collaboration with the Wesley Fellowship, Ilkeston, 1995. pp.31. ISBN 0 95163 324 4.

28. Herbert McGonigle. *Scriptural Holiness: The Wesleyan Distinctive.* The 1995 Maynard James Memorial Lecture. Moorley's Print & Publishing in collaboration with The Flame Trust, Ilkeston, 1995.

29. Charles H. Goodwin. *An Evangelistical Pastorate: the unresolved dilemma in Wesleyan concepts of ministry and church growth.* Shearsby: The Wesley Fellowship, 1995.

30. Paul Taylor, ed. *Wesley Pieces: Conference and Other Papers 1995.*[21] Ilkeston: The Wesley Fellowship with Moorleys Print & Publishing, 1996. pp.56. ISBN 0951 16332 5 2.

31. Peter Gentry. *Francis Asbury – the Wesley of America.* Ilkeston: Moorleys Print & Publishing, 1996. pp.15. ISBN 0 86071 480 2.

32. Charles Goodwin. The *Methodist Pentecost: The Wesleyan Holiness Revival 1758-1763.* Merlin Methodist Monograph No.4. Ilkeston: Moorleys Print & Publishing in Association with the Wesley Fellowship, 1996. pp.38. ISBN 0 951633 26 0.

33. *Colin N. Peckham. *John Wesley's Understanding of Human Infirmities.* [Occasional Paper No. 10.] Ilkeston: The Wesley Fellowship, 1997.

34. William Parkes. *Phoebe Palmer: Organised for Revival.* The 1997 Maynard James Memorial Lecture. Ilkeston: Moorleys Print & Publishing in association with The Flame Trust and The Wesley Fellowship, 1998.

---

[21] This publication, *Wesley Pieces: Conference and other Papers*, contains the following articles based on papers read to the 1995 Wesley Fellowship residential conference: 1. Herbert McGonigle, 'Wesleyan Arminianism', p. 5; 2. William Parkes, 'The Love-Feast', pp. 6-7; 3. William Parkes, 'Elizabeth Ann Evans-"Dinah Morris" her "Derby Faith" Portrait', pp. 9-15; 4. David Guy, 'The Influence of John Wesley on William & Catherine Booth', pp. 16-26; 5. Stephen Hatcher, 'The Primitive Methodist Experience of Holiness', pp. 27-35; and 6. John Andrews, 'John Wesley and the Translation of German Hymns', pp. 36-42. Also two sermons: 1. Colin Peckham, 'Sanctified Through and Through', pp. 44-52; and 2. Leslie Evans, 'Paul's Plan of Progress in Philippians 3: 12-16', pp. 53-56.

35. Paul Taylor, ed. *Wesleyan Perspectives: Papers Presented to The Wesley Fellowship in 1998.*[22] Ilkeston: Moorleys Print & Publishing in association with the Wesley Fellowship, 1998. A4 format, pp.34. ISBN 0 9516332 9 5.

36. Charles Goodwin. *Cries of Anguish – Shouts of Praise: The Development of Wesleyan Revivalism 1739-1818.* Originally published by the author, a Wesley Fellowship member, as Merlin Methodist Monograph, No 2, at Cannock, Staffordshire, 1994; Republished, with permission, by the Wesley Fellowship, Ilkeston, 1999. pp.62.

37. *Ian Randall. *Pathway of Power: Keswick and the Reshaping of Wesleyan Holiness 1875-1905.* [Occasional Paper No. 11.] Shearsby: The Wesley Fellowship, 1999. pp.28. ISBN 0 9516332 8 7.

38. *Paul Smith. *John Wesley: Preacher of the Gospel.* [Occasional Paper No. 12.] Shearsby: The Wesley Fellowship, 2000. pp.20. ISBN 0 9537473 0 1.

39. Gentry, Peter W. *John Fletcher and the Introduction of the "Baptism" Motif in the Wesleyan concept of sanctification.* The Maynard James Memorial Lectures No. 11. North Petherton, Somerset: Grace Wesleyan Trust, 2000.[23]

40. Gentry, Peter W. *Inner Light and Warmed Heart: A study of the contrasts and similarities between the Quakers and the early Methodists.* Western-super-Mare: Peter W. Gentry, 2001.[24]

41. *Deirdre Brower. *Susanna Wesley: Practical Theologian.* [Occasional Paper No. 13.] Shearsby: The Wesley Fellowship, 2001. ISBN 0 9537473 1 X. pp.19.

42. Paul Taylor, ed. *Wesley Papers: Papers presented to The Wesley Fellowship Conference in 2000.*[25] Ilkeston: The Wesley Fellowship in

---

[22] This publication, *Wesleyan Perspectives*, contains the following articles based on papers read to Wesley Fellowship meetings during 1998: 1. Trevor Staniforth, 'John Wesley's Puritan Roots'; 2. John Dolan, 'The Origins and Early Characteristics of the Independent Methodist Movement'; Brian Barber, 'Revival Seeds'.

[23] Although this paper by Peter Gentry was not read to a meeting of the Wesley Fellowship, it was discussed, reviewed, and distributed at WF meetings.

[24] This paper by Peter W. Gentry was not read to a meeting of the Wesley Fellowship, but it was noted, discussed and distributed at meetings of the WF.

[25] This publication, *Wesley Papers*, contains the following articles based on papers read to the Wesley Fellowship residential conference held at Cliff College in 2000: 1. John E. Colwell, 'Offending in Many Things: A Comparison of John Wesley and Thomas Aquinas on the nature of sin in the believer', pp. 3-14; 2. William T. Graham, 'Pupils in the Gospel: The Education of John Wesley's

Association with Moorley's Print & Publishing, 2002. pp.98. ISBN 0 9537473 0 1.

43. *John M. Haley. *John Wesley: The Means of Grace and the Holy Life Today.* [Occasional Paper No. 14.] Shearsby: The Wesley Fellowship, 2003. ISBN 0 9837473 2 8. pp.28.

44. A.M. Roger. *Revival: The Revelation of a Holy God.* The 2003 Maynard James Memorial Lecture, presented in April 2003 at Zion Church, Handsworth, Birmingham, in association with the Wesley Fellowship. Edinburgh: The Faith Mission, n.d. [first published in four parts in *The Flame,* July 2003-April 2004]

45. Ian M. Randall. *Entire Devotion to God: Wesleyan Holiness and British Overseas Mission in the Early Twentieth Century.* Shearsby: The Wesley Fellowship, 1998.

46. *John M. Hayley. *John Wesley, The Means of Grace and the Holy Life Today.* Occasional Paper No. 14. Shearsby: The Wesley Fellowship, 2003.

47. Paul Taylor. *Sleepers Awake! The Gospel and Postmodernism.* The 2004 Maynard James Memorial Lecture. Weston-Super-Mare: The Flame Trust and The Wesley Fellowship, 2004.

48. *John Wood. *The Peculiar People: A Nineteenth Century Methodist Off-Shoot in Essex.* [Occasional Paper No. 15.] Shearsby: The Wesley Fellowship, 2004. ISBN 0953774733 6. pp.28.

49. *John M. Hayley. *'A Little Body of Experimental and Practical Divimity': Hymns in the Wesleyan-Arminian Tradition.* [Occasional Paper No. 16.] Shearsby: The Wesley Fellowship, 2005.

50. Herbert B. McGonigle. *John Wesley's Arminian Theology: An Introduction.* Second Edition; Revised and Reset. Shearsby: The Wesley Fellowship, 2005.

51. Ian Randall. *The Bible is Central: Cliff College and the Evangelical Tradition.* The 2006 Maynard James Memorial Lecture. Weston-Super-Mare: The Flame Trust and The Wesley Fellowship, 2006.

52. *Paul S. Taylor. *Charles Wesley: Evangelist; Christ for All – All for Christ.* Occasional Paper No. 17. Shearsby: The Wesley Fellowship, 2007.

53. Paul Taylor and Peter Gentry. *Bold as a Lion: The Life of John Cennick (1718-1755) Moravian Evangelist.* Leicester: Life Publications, 2007.

Preachers', pp. 15-70; 3. William Parkes, 'Lorenzo Dow 1777-1834: "the Eccentric Cosmopolite"', pp. 71-86; and 4. Geoffrey Fewkes, 'John Wesley and Reader Harris: Stages in Salvation', pp. 87-98.

54. *Herbert Boyd McGonigle. *A Burning and Shining Light: The Life and Ministry of William Bramwell*. [Occasional Paper No. 18.] Sheffield: The Wesley Fellowship, 2009.

55. Harold E. Moore. *Make the Mountains Flow: The Holy Spirit in the Hymns of Charles Wesley*. Sheffield: The Wesley Fellowship in Partnership with The League of Prayer, 2010.

56. Trevor Staniforth. *The Methodist Pentecost: Personal Testimonies and Eyewitness Accounts of Revival in the 1760s and the Doctrine of Entire Sanctification*. Sheffield: The Wesley Fellowship in partnership with The League of Prayer, 2010.

57. Paul S. Taylor. *The Fountain of Life: John Wesley and The Holy Spirit*. Sheffield: The Wesley Fellowship in Partnership with The League of Prayer, 2010.

58. Paul S. Taylor. *James Montgomery: A man for all people*. History Today. Leominster: Day One Publications, 2010.

59. *Peter W. Gentry. *Methodism and Messiah: Reflections on John and Charles Wesley, the early Methodists and George Frederic Handel's great oratorio*. Occasional Paper No. 20. Sheffield: The Wesley Fellowship, 2011.

60. Herbert Boyd McGonigle. *Christianity or Deism?: John Wesley's Response to John Taylor's denial of the Doctrine of Original Sin*. Ilkeston: The Wesley Fellowship, 2012.

61. Paul S. Taylor. *John Newton: Evangelical Spirituality and Social Concern*. Occasional Paper No. 21. Sheffield: The Wesley Fellowship, 2012.

62. Andrew J. Cheatle. *William Sangster: Heir of John Wesley?* Sheffield: The Wesley Fellowship, 2013.

63. *William T. Graham. *"Sent by my Lord, on you I call": Reflections on the Genesis of John Wesley's Preaching*. Occasional Paper No. 22. Sheffield: The Wesley Fellowship, 2013.

Note: The projected 'Occasional Paper No. 19', a fine paper by the late Mr E. Alan Rose entitled "A History of the New Methodist Connexion", that he read at the Wesley Fellowship meeting held at Zion Church of the Nazarene, Handsworth, Birmingham, on Saturday 4 November 2006, does not appear in this listing, because it was never actually published, mainly because Alan felt he was unable to get the text finalised to his satisfaction, and so the WF never received his manuscript copy.

Preface

When I was asked to give the Didsbury Lectures in 2002, I didn't think twice about the area I should choose – it was going to be about John Wesley! I had been lecturing in the College for twenty-six years and I had covered the whole series of Church History, theology and other subjects, but Wesley Studies remained my favourite. Back in 1976 when I joined the College, Wesley Studies was given to me and I had read widely in that subject and made many a visit to the places concerned. All across England, Ireland, Scotland and Wales; I had made many visits to all the Wesley sites but it is to Epworth that I had gone again and again. I had made regular visits to Epworth, the home of the Wesleys, some seventy times (!) and I always enjoyed the next one. At the same time I was busy collecting Wesleyana pottery and the one shop I visited in Epworth was that owned by people called Dilys and Bert Oldfield and I picked up a lot from them. I had Wesleyana displaying itself across six shelves in my study and it was there for General Superintendents, Presidents of Nazarene Universities, District Superintendents, pastors, students and people of all ranks who had come to look at the display.

When one is choosing a subject like John Wesley studies, care must be taken to opt for studies that would have seemed relevant to Wesley. For most of his life John Wesley held to a thorough grasp of scripture and it seemed to me to be a proper place to begin. Writing to John Newton on May 14, 1765, Wesley placed an emphasis on the year 1730. 'In 1730 I began to be *homo unius libri*, to study no book (comparatively) like the Bible.'[26] In *Farther Thoughts on Separation from the Church,* written in London, December 11, 1789, he avowed, 'From a child I was taught to love and reverence the Scriptures, the oracles of God.'[27] In a decade stretching more than sixty years, he never wavered from this absolute opinion. In sermons, letters, tracts, biblical expositions, journal and diaries, he held to this conviction from start to finish. All his life he believed that the scriptures was the only form of worship and he held to it with conviction and passion. In a long letter written to Henry Venn, June 22, 1765, he spelt it out in terms of reading the Bible. 'I believe

---

[26] John Wesley, *Letters*, Vol. 4, p.299.
[27] John Wesley, *The Works of John Wesley*, Vol. 13, p.272.

all the Bible as far as I understand it, and am ready to be convinced. If I am an heretic, I became such by reading the Bible.'[28]
Another of John Wesley's life-long passions was the opinion that salvation of God was for all. Returning to England early in 1738 his opinion in an autobiographical memorandum was, 'I want that faith which none can have without knowing that he had it. For whosoever had it is from sin .... he is freed from fear .... and he is freed from doubt.'[29] This was written on February 1, 1738, and fifty-two years later he gave the same advice at the close of the sermon, *On the Wedding Garment*, printed on March 26, 1790. 'This he hath proclaimed to them in his word, together with the terms of salvation revealed by the Son of his love, who gave his own life that they that believe in him might have everlasting life.'[30] In fifty years John Wesley was adamant that the salvation purchased by Christ must be sought and found and preached and proclaimed to every repentant sinner. All his life he devoted to this service and he preached and proclaimed it until Wednesday, February 22, 1791, when he delivered his last sermon at Leatherhead in Surrey, on one of his favourite passages. 'The kingdom of heaven is at hand; repent, and believe the Gospel.' [31] One week before his death he charged his hearers to seek and find the Lord and walk in His ways.

Another of John Wesley's favourite topics was the way he viewed evangelism. As the work progressed in his societies he saw his work as that of primarily an evangelist. He wrote to 'John Smith' in March 22, 1748. 'Whenever I see one or a thousand men running into hell .... I will stop them if I can: as a minister of Christ, I will beseech in His name to turn back and be reconciled to God.'[32] On August 6, 1777, he wrote to Alexander Mather. 'Give me one hundred preachers who fear nothing but sin and desire nothing but God, and I care not a straw whether they be clergymen or laymen, such alone will shake the gates of hell and set the kingdom of God upon the earth.'[33] When John Wesley was in Bristol in 1739 he preached for the first time out of doors and he continued preaching in all places until he was eighty-eight. All his life he was a preacher and it has been said he preached sermons inside churches but much more outside.

---

[28] John Wesley, *Letters,* Vol. 4, p.216.
[29] John Wesley, Vol. 18, p.216.
[30] John Wesley, *Works [BE],* Vol. 4, 148.
[31] John Wesley, *Works [BE],* Vol. 26, 291.
[32] John Wesley, *Works [BE],* Vol. 26:291.
[33] John Wesley, *Letters,* Vol. 6, p.272.

Finally, Christian holiness was a concern of John Wesley's all his life. The year 1729 marked the beginning of real religion and from that time Wesley began to preach sanctification as the goal of the Christian life. 'In 1729, two young men, reading the Bible, saw that they could not be saved without holiness .... God then thrust them out, utterly against their will, to raise a holy people.'[34] On September 15, 1790, he replied to a letter from Robert Carr Brackenbury. 'This doctrine is the grand depositum which God has lodged with the people called Methodists; and for the sake of propagating this chiefly He appeared to have raised us up.'[35] On November 26, 1790, John Wesley wrote to Dr. Adam Clarke and gave his opinion on Local Preachers and Leaders. 'If we can prove that any of our Local Preachers or Leaders, can directly or indirectly, speak against it, let him be a Local Preacher or Leader no longer. I doubt whether he should continue in the society. Because he that could speak thus in our congregation cannot be an honest man.'[36] From 1729 until 1790, there was no let up on the doctrine of holiness – a space of sixty-one years. Add to them the many sermons, lectures, writing in letters on sanctification, *A Plain Account of Christian Perfection,* and the increasing number of men and women holding to Christian holiness in their own lives, meant that for John Wesley this part of Christian perfection must be sought by all believers.

Before faculty, students and college staff and visitors, it was an honour to give the Lectures. I had lectured in the College since 1976 and for fifteen years, I conducted the College lectures on Christian holiness. As I prepared the 2002 Lectures for printing, I remember so well the quantity of questions facing me each evening. I hope the faculty and students were well supplied with answers! I hope that students past and present will find the Lectures helpful and that many more will be asking questions.

While I was preparing the Lectures, I asked Bill Graham to prepare a Foreword. Bill agreed and he sent me over thirty pages! He delved into my lectures and prepared for me a whole host of his writing and sent it to me. I was overwhelmed and he must have spent hours and hours going through my writings and pulling out everything that was needful. He searched my writings and gave to me a catalogue of everything that was for me 'To Know One Thing', a catalogue of everything I wrote about forty years ago and since!

---

[34] John Wesley, *Works*, Vol. 8, p.244.
[35] John Wesley, *Letters,* Vol. 8, p.238.
[36] John Wesley, *Works,* Vol. 13, p.105.

- and some things I had forgotten! Jeanne and I came from Leeds Church of the Nazarene in September 1976 and it wasn't long before we met Bill and Lorraine and we have been the best of friends ever since. That was in 1976 and now it's 2020 - forty-four years ago! Jeanne has now been gone three years and if she was living now, she would be delighted. On behalf of Jeanne, this Foreword is deeply unsurpassable. Well done, Bill, and thank you for reading all my writings!

LECTURE 1
JOHN WESLEY AND SCRIPTURE

When John Wesley once described himself as 'a man of one book', he was referring to his life-long conviction that the Scriptures were the oracles of the one true God. While this conviction was undoubtedly clarified and intensified by a lifetime of studying the Bible and being engaged in Christian apologetics for half a century, it began in the literary and pietistic atmosphere of his Epworth rectory home. Near the end of his life he recalled these early doctrinal impressions. 'From a child I was taught to love and reverence the Scripture, the oracles of God.' Throughout a long life of preaching, writing, publishing and engaging in theological debate with friends and opponents alike, John Wesley never deviated from that conviction that holy Scripture is the word of God. In it the God and Father of Jesus Christ is revealed, through its evangel we hear the gospel of grace and salvation and by the mediation of the Holy Spirit it has inherent power to build believers up in faith and holiness. This chapter will explore three areas of John Wesley's understanding and use of Scripture. First that he was an heir of the well-established Anglican tradition concerning the Scriptures; second, his practical application of Scripture in preaching and pastoral counsel, and, third, the principles of biblical interpretation that he practised.

John Wesley: Heir of the Anglican Tradition

When John Wesley confessed that he had been trained up from a child to reverence Scripture as God's word, he enlarged on those influences that emanated from his parents' reasoning and example.

> From a child I was taught.... to esteem the primitive Fathers, the writers of the first three centuries. Next after the primitive church, I esteemed our own, the Church of England, as the most scriptural national Church in the world. I therefore not only assented to all the doctrines, but observed all the rubric

> in the Liturgy; and that with all possible exactness, even at the peril of my life. [37]

Although John Wesley does not name in so many words the precise books that his parents, Samuel and Susanna Wesley read themselves and encouraged their children to read, yet there is clear evidence concerning Samuel's preference for the best interpreters of Scripture. In his, *Advice to a Young Clergyman*, he strongly urged the constant reading and study of Scripture and then gave his opinion on ancient and contemporary Christian writers. The First and Second Letters of Clement, the Letters of Ignatius and the writings of Irenaeus, Justin, Clement of Alexander, Tertullian and Cyprian are all recommended. Athanasius, Basil of Caesarea and Chrysostom are especially recommended while Jerome and Augustine are of lesser value. Of the Reformation period Samuel Wesley acknowledged he had not read much in Martin Luther, Melanchthon he reckoned ingenuous, Calvin should be read with caution, Martin Bucer was moderate in his opinions and Erasmus was useful. It is, however, among the 16th and 17th century Anglican writers that Wesley finds most to recommend. The writings of Bishop Jewel, Cranmer and Ridley are outstandingly good and Richard Hooker is unanswerable. The works of Archbishops William Laud and John Tillitson are commended as well as those of some eleven Bishops, including John Pearson, Gilbert Burnet, Thomas Ken, George Bull and Jeremy Taylor. Other Anglican divines warmly endorsed were Henry Hammond, John Lightfoot and John Selden. In this galaxy of Anglican luminaries, Bishop John Pearson was singled out for special commendation. Samuel Wesley asserted that Pearson's writings on Ignatius of Antioch and on the Creed 'ought to be in every Clergyman's study in England,' a commendation later endorsed by his son, John Wesley.[38]

---

[37] John Wesley, *Works*, Vol. 13, p.272.

[38] Wesley wrote to a ministerial candidate at Oxford, 'In order to be well acquainted with the doctrines of Christianity, you need but one book, (besides the Bible) – Bishop Pearson on the Creed … It is a library.... It is a library in one volume.' *Letters*, Vol. 4, p.243.

Samuel Wesley's reading list is a good guide to the Fathers, theologians, bishops and apologists that he undoubtedly recommended to John. His penchant was for the Eastern Church Fathers and the Anglican theologians of the 16th and 17th centuries. In doing this he was emphasising what might be called the theological method of the Anglican scholars he rated so highly.[39] Henry McAdoo has argued convincingly that after the acknowledged authority of Scripture, the appeal of Anglicanism to the Church Fathers was the essential characteristic of its theological scholarship from Richard Hooker to William Law.[40] Samuel Wesley's recommendations to John were not in vain. Between the years 1725 and 1735, John Wesley's Oxford *Diaries*, a large number of the Anglican writers recommended by his father are included. The *Diaries* further indicate that not only did John Wesley personally read these books but he introduced many of them in the meetings of the Oxford 'Holy Club' and from many of them he subsequently published extracts. In addition to these Anglican writers endorsed by his father, John also read privately, and in the 'Holy Club', many more Church of England writers, especially those who emphasised what he was beginning to label 'heart religion'. These included Richard Allestree, Francis Atterbury, Isaac Barrow, Thomas Deacon, George Herbert, Anthony Horneck and Robert Nelson. All these writers, with varying degrees of emphasis, argued Holy Scripture to be the primary authority for Christian faith and practice. In addition they also embodied the Anglican hermeneutical trilogy, with their appeal to Scripture, reason and tradition. For many of them, and certainly for their disciple John Wesley, the Scriptures were not just an authority of equal value with reason and tradition, but rather occupying the place of supreme authority. Reason and tradition often illuminated and illustrated the authority of Scripture but never represented an equal, much less a superior, authority.

Among the Anglican divines recommended by Samuel Wesley and read by John Wesley in his Oxford days, were John Pearson, Henry

---

[39] T. Jackson, *The Life of The Rev. Charles Wesley*. Vol. 2, pp.500-534.

[40] H. R. McAdoo, *The Spirit of Anglicanism*, London,1965, especially chapters IX and X.

Hammond and Gilbert Burnet. These writers represented the authentic Anglican tradition and their stance on Scripture is clear and unequivocal. Hammond (1605-1660), became an acknowledged expert in the history, theology and practice of the Church of England and published, in particular, two pieces of outstanding practical and exegetical Anglican apologias. The first was his, *Practical Catechism,* (1664), followed later by, *Paraphrases and Annotations on the New Testament,* (1664). This latter work set a high standard in the field of biblical interpretation. Hammond translated the entire New Testament into English and proposed to make it the text on which the, *Paraphrases and Annotations,* would be based. After consulting other scholars, he printed the authorised translation instead but wrote many notes on marginal alterations. He had carefully compared all the available New Testament Greek MSS and drew attention to those variant readings which he believed were superior. Drawing on the language and literature of the first Christian century, Hammond employed it to help interpret the biblical text. His argument was that Scripture was the inspired word of God and that it required the meticulous study of the original text to bring out its precise meaning. John Pearson (1613-1686) earned his reputation for his massive learning, especially his linguistic expertise and his unrivalled knowledge of the Church Fathers. He was a leading contributor to the six-volume, *Biblia Sacra Polyglotta,* published in the 1650's and the author of the definitive exposition and defence of the Letters of Ignatius. It was, however, his *Exposition of the Creed,* (1659) that established him as the outstanding apologist of the Church of England. With an admirably lucid style Pearson explained in great depth all twelve articles of the Apostles' Creed. Drawing on his unrivalled knowledge of the Church Fathers, he illustrated his arguments with copious references from Patristic writings, yet the main thrust of the, *Exposition,* was that it embodied Scripture truth. Speaking of the dogmatic statements found in the Creed, Pearson confessed his unshakeable convictions about them because they represented the teaching of Holy Scripture.

> Although those things which I am ready to affirm be not apparent to me sense, so that I cannot say that I see them;

> although they be not evident to my understanding of themselves, nor appear unto me true by the virtue of any natural and necessary cause, so that I cannot say I have any proper knowledge or science of them; yet seeing they are certainly contained in the scriptures, the writings of the blessed apostles and prophets; seeing those apostles and prophets were endued with miraculous power from above, and immediately inspired with the Holy Ghost, and consequently what they delivered was not the word of the man, but of God himself; seeing God is of that universal knowledge and infinite wisdom, that it is impossible he should be deceived; of that indefectible holiness and transcendent rectitude, that it is not imaginable he should intend to deceive any man, and, consequently whatsoever he hath delivered for a truth, must be necessarily and infallibly true; I readily and steadily assent to them as most certain truths, and am as fully, and absolutely, and more concerningly persuaded of them, than of any thing I see or know.[41]

Pearson's work is an admirable example of that kind of 17th Century Anglican apologia that relies on the interpretive trilogy of Scripture, reason and tradition, but clearly for Pearson, Scripture is authoritative in a way that tradition and reason is not. Gilbert Burnet (1643-1715) published his celebrated work, *An Exposition of the Thirty-Nine Articles,* in 1699, and it became the most widely read and quoted work on the *Articles*. Article VI of the Thirty-Nine was entitled, 'Of the Sufficiency of the holy Scriptures for salvation,' and part of it read: 'Holy Scripture containeth all things necessary to salvation: so that whatsoever is not read therein, nor may be proved thereby, is not to be required of any man, that it should be believed as an article of the faith or be thought requisite or necessary to salvation.'

Burnet pointed out that following the earlier *Articles* on God and Christ, this Article was concerned with showing what the rule of faith is, where it can be found and with whom it is lodged. Although the Church of Rome accepted the Scriptures as of divine inspiration, that

---

[41] John Pearson, *An Exposition of the Creed,* London, 1823, p.22.

Church also believes that many other things were spoken orally by the Apostles. These 'additional' teachings, it is claimed, have been faithfully transmitted by the Roman Church and are to be received with 'the same Submission and Respect' that is paid to the canonical writings. The Church of Rome further claims that 'these traditions are conveyed down infallibly to us,' and constitute 'an infallible Authority lodged by Christ with His Church.' Burnet protests against this Roman defence of tradition.

> We on the contrary affirm, that the Scriptures are a complete Rule of Faith, and that the whole Christian religion is contained in them, and nowhere else; and although we make great use of Tradition, especially that which is most Ancient and nearest the Source, to help us to a clear understanding of the Scriptures; yet as to matters of faith we reject all oral tradition, as an incompetent means of conveying down Doctrines to us, and we refuse to receive any Doctrine, that is not either expressly contained in Scripture, or clearly proved from it.[42]

These three Anglican defences of the divine inspiration, authority and infallibility of Holy Scripture were representative of the many like-minded theological writings that John Wesley studied carefully at Oxford in the years 1725-1735. These writings confirmed the understanding of Holy Scripture he had imbibed from his father's instruction at Epworth. The Church of England unequivocally made the Holy Scriptures its rule of faith and Wesley was eager to make the same declaration. As he prepared for ordination in 1725 he approached the *Articles* with careful consideration. Entering Holy Orders required subscription to the, *Thirty-Nine Articles,* and in correspondence with his mother Susannah, he expressed his doubts about the wording of Article XVII on predestination.[43] He read a number of books dealing with the *Articles* and eventually he was able to sign his allegiance to them with conviction. When he was questioned on this matter twenty years later, he was able to reply:

---

[42] Gilbert Burnet, *An Exposition of the Thirty-Nine Articles of the Church of* England, London, 1699, p.72.

[43] John Wesley, *Works [BE]*, Vol. 25, p.176.

> In saying 'I teach the doctrines of the Church of England,' I do, and always did, mean I teach the doctrines which are comprised in those Articles and Homilies to which all the clergy of the Church of England solemnly profess to assent, and that in their plain, unforced, grammatical meaning.[44]

In his Oxford days John Wesley was laying a foundation of complete reliance upon Scripture as the sure word of God upon which he would build the remainder of his long ministry. There is clear evidence in his writings that as he wrestled with the important questions of the inspiration and interpretation of Scripture, he was greatly influenced by the biblical and patristic scholars he had studied. Returning from Savannah early in 1738 he composed a kind of spiritual Memorandum in which he reviewed his spiritual pilgrimage, especially with reference to his understanding of salvation. He wrote of how 'for many years' he had been 'tossed by various winds of doctrine' as he pondered the biblical question, 'What must I do to be saved?' He thought the Scripture's answer was, 'Keep the commandments, believe, hope, love.'[45] This was a period of intense spiritual crisis in John Wesley's life. His time in Savannah had left him spiritually deflated for he had gone on that missionary enterprise, as he admitted, as much to save his own soul. His question now was a sotcriological question – how can I be saved? In many ways this soteriological interest would dominate the rest of his life. Many years later, with the days of spiritual uncertainty long behind him, and when he was caught up in the great mission of his life, he would confess that pursuing salvation was still the dominating interest of his life. 'I want to know one thing, the way to heaven.'

Continuing his reflective evaluation, he wrote of how he had been warned against putting too much of an emphasis on 'outward works, as the papists do,' or, alternately, over-stressing faith to the exclusion of works. Writing on a January day in 1738 he was sure he had not distorted this balance of faith and works, though in the months to come

---

[44] John Wesley, *Letters*, Vol. 2, p.57.
[45] John Wesley, *Works [BE],* Vol. 18, p.212.

he would revise that judgement. Then he recalled how he had fallen among 'some Lutheran and Calvinist authors,' and their 'overgrown fear of Popery' so magnified faith that the rest of the commandments were eclipsed. None of these Lutheran and Calvinist writers are named and although his Oxford *Diaries* between 1725 and 1735 have a meticulous record of his reading in those years, no obvious candidates are included. It may be that his reference to 'many years ago' points to his reading prior to 1725, the year in which the *Diaries* began. He described this earlier period as a labyrinth in which he was 'utterly lost,' being unable to reconcile what he thought were the opposing claims of faith and works. But help was at hand and it came from three Anglican theologians in particular, Bishops Beveridge and Taylor and Robert Nelson. Wesley recorded that these writers had given him some relief from the 'well-meaning, wrong-headed Germans.'[46] William Beveridge (1637-1667) was an acknowledged expert in Patristic studies and at Oxford Wesley had read his great work, *Codex Canonum Ecclesiae Primitivae*, and taken it with him to Savannah. More significantly he had Beveridge's, One *Hundred and Fifty Discourses,* as early as 1726. A year earlier he had read Jeremy Taylor's, *Rule and Exercise*, and this confirms how both these writers, Beveridge and Taylor, had helped Wesley out of the confusion caused by the Lutheran and Calvinist writings. As he had read Beveridge and Taylor in the years 1725 and 1736, then his reading of the Lutheran and Calvinist authors predated these years. He also named Robert Nelson as another helpful guide at this period. Nelson (1656-1715) was a Nonjuror and a layman and the bulk of his writings were with the religion of the heart. He was one of Wesley's favourite authors and the *Diaries* show that he had read five of Nelson's writings, *A Companion for the Festivals and The Practice of True Devotion*. Albert Outler suggests that Wesley also numbered among his mentors Anglican writers like Thomas Ken, John Kettlewell and George Smalridge. The common interest of these writers was 'their rootage in a Christian tradition more primitive than

---

[46] John Wesley *Works [BE]*, Vol. 18, p.212.

the corruption of the 'papists' or the exaggerations of the 'protestants.''[47]

Wesley recalled how these Anglican theologians gave him an account of Christianity that was consistent with Scripture and reason. The difficulty was that they were not always agreed in their hermeneutical principles. Then he discovered what he termed a 'sure rule for interpreting Scripture.' This was Vincent of Lerins', *Canon*, which Wesley understood as, 'the consensus of antiquity: that which has been believed by everyone, everywhere and always.' But this discovery was a mixed blessing. Directing his attention to antiquity, that is, the Primitive church, Wesley found himself in a place where, in his own words, he was 'making antiquity a co-ordinate rather than subordinate rule with Scripture.' It was in his Oxford years 1720-35, while he was taken up with this admiration for the writers of the first four centuries, that he began to read the Continental Mystics. Their portrayal of what union with God means made everything else appear 'mean, flat and insipid.' At this period Wesley was strongly influenced by William Law who introduced him to the Theologia Germanica, and he also discovered the writings of influential Mystics including Michael Molinos, Archbishop Fenelon and Francis de Sales. But this enthusiasm for Law's mysticism soon began to evaporate as Wesley concluded it was not the religion of Christ and his apostles. Although he was not sure of exactly how or when he was 'rescued' from Mysticism, he had returned to the right way and now warned that the mystics are 'the most dangerous enemies' of Christianity.[48]

Although this private memorandum was mainly concerned with John Wesley's search for spiritual assurance, that search was bound up with another – how to find the best means of understanding Holy Scripture. He was sure that the Bible alone taught 'the way of salvation,' and as he wrestled with Lutheran and Calvinist exegesis, the excitement generated by the renaissance of Patristic studies and the claims of

[47] Albert Outler, *John Wesley*, Oxford, 1964, p.45.
[48] John Wesley, *Works [BE]*, Vol. 18, p.213.

mystical experience, this son of the Epworth rectory eventually returned to his Anglican moorings. From a child, he claimed, he had been taught 'to love and reverence the Scripture, the oracles of God,' and as he surveyed nearly twenty years of his pilgrimage, he singled out Bishops Beveridge and Taylor and Robert Nelson as the best guides in his search for 'the scripture was' of salvation. In the years to come he would certainly go further than any of his mentors in proclaiming and defending the full, sufficient and final authority of Holy Scripture in all matters of faith and practice, but he never forgot those who had been his most trustworthy guides. When he assumed the leadership of the little group at Oxford soon to be known as 'Methodists,' he made the reading and study of Scripture their main employment. Wesley later described the members of the 'Holy Club' as 'zealous members of the Church of England' who were fully committed to all her doctrines and were also 'zealous observers' of the University Statutes. Then he added that these disciplines were freely accepted for conscience sake. 'But they observed neither these nor anything else any further than they conceived it bound upon them by their one book, the Bible; it being their one desire and design to be downright Bible-Christians.'

Years later he enlarged on this and linked the Oxford Methodists with his followers fifty years on. And the link was that 'Methodists,' from their first inception, were, and still are, the people of 'the Book.'

> From the very beginning, from the time that four young men united together, each of them *homo unius libri* – a man of one book. God taught them all to make his 'Word a lantern unto their feet, and a light in all their paths.' They had one, and only one rule of judgment with regard to all their tempers, words, and actions, namely, the oracles of God. They were one and all determined to be *Bible-Christians.* They were continually reproached for this very thing; some terming them in derision *Bible-bigots*; others *Bible-moths* – feeding, they said, upon the Bible as moths do upon cloth. And indeed unto this day it is their constant endeavour to think and speak as the oracles of God.[49]

---

[49] John Wesley, *Works*, Vol. 8, p.348.

Clearly John Wesley was not in the least offended by epithets like 'Bible-bigots' and 'Bible-moths' being applied to himself and his followers. Rather he seemed to accept these derisive descriptions with pride for they magnified the very thing he wanted England to know – the Methodists loved Holy Scripture. It is hardly surprising then that he saw those Oxford days as the time when the study of the Bible was the chief occupation of the little group of which he was the spiritual leader. In his own pilgrimage of faith he selected 1729 in particular as the year when he began 'not only to read, but to study, the Bible, as the one, the only standard of truth, and the only model of pure religion.'[50] Sixteen years later he was of the same persuasion in his correspondence with 'John Smith,' a leading Churchman. He pointed out that the apostles defended their assertions 'by the written Word. You and I are to do the same. Without such proof I ought no more to have believed St. Peter himself than St. Peter's (pretended) successor.... I receive the written Word as the whole and sole rule of my faith.'[51] Twenty years after, in 1766, he was making the same confession about his unreserved commitment to Holy Scripture. 'My ground is the Bible. Yes I am a Bible-bigot. I follow it in all things, both great and small.'[52] A decade later he declared his belief in the infallibility of the Scriptures even more pointedly. Reviewing a book by Soame Jenyns, he thought the author a fine writer but confessed he could not make up his mind whether he was a Christian, a Deist or an Atheist.

> If he is a Christian, he betrays his own cause by averring that 'all Scripture is not given by inspiration of God, but the writers of it were sometimes left to themselves, and consequently made some mistakes.' Nay, if there be any mistakes in the Bible, there may as well be a thousand. If there be one falsehood in that book, it did not come from the God of truth.[53]

---

[50] John Wesley, *Works*, Vol. 11, p.367.
[51] John Wesley, *Letters*, Vol. 2, p.44.
[52] John Wesley, *Journal*, Vol. 5, p.169.
[53] John Wesley, *Journal*, Vol. 6, p.117.

John Wesley's writings contain overwhelming proof that throughout his long life and ministry he never deviated in his conviction about the Bible. For him it was quite simply, 'the oracles of God,' and on all its pages he saw the stamp of the divine imprimatur. Even before his Aldersgate 'heart-warming' of May 24, 1738, Wesley affirmed his determination to abide by what the Bible said. Following a conversation with Peter Bohler on the nature of saving faith, he wrote: 'The next morning I began the Greek Testament again, resolving to abide by the Law and the Testimony.'[54] From this determination he never wavered and many years later he wrote: 'I will speak for one. After having sought for truth with some diligence for half a century I am at this day hardly sure of anything but what I learn from the Bible. Nay, I positively affirm I know nothing else so certainly that I would dare to stake my salvation upon it.'[55]

John Wesley's Use of Scripture

From this survey of how John Wesley asserted his life-long conviction about the inspiration and authority of Holy Scripture, it is time to look and see what this meant in practice. How did he use the Scriptures? It is one thing for a theologian to declare his belief in the divine origin of Scripture but the test is – to what use does he put the Scripture in the construction of his theological system? John Wesley wrote many theological works and they need to be examined to see if his claims about Scripture are borne out. In addition, he was the spiritual leader of thousands of people who looked to him for guidance in the things of God. To help his Methodist people, Wesley instituted Class and Band meetings, Quarterly meetings, Love Feasts, Watch-Night services and other means of grace. What part did the Scriptures play in the practice of these institutions?

At one level, this question about how John Wesley used the Bible in theological construction and pastoral practice is very easily answered.

---

[54] John Wesley, *Works [BE]*, Vol. 18, p.232.
[55] John Wesley, *Works [BE]*, Vol. 2, p.289.

We need only look at the number of times the Scriptures are quoted in sermons, letters, treaties and apologias. Quite simply, his writings abound with direct quotations from and allusions and references to, the Word of God. What he said in 1784 in answer to a question was typical of how he constantly referred to the Bible both for his own edification and his people's. Discussing how the land was over-run with ungodliness he asked: 'By what means are we to avoid the being carried away by the overflowing stream of dissipation?' He answered his own question. 'It is not difficult for those who believe the Scripture to give an answer to this question. Now I really believe the Bible to be the Word of God; and on that supposition I answer: the radical cure...is the "faith that worketh by love."'[56]

Between 1746 and 1788 John Wesley published scores of his sermons. Many of these were published under the title, *Sermons on Several Occasions*, others were published singly and some were published in his *Arminian Magazine*, which he launched in 1788. Dipping into these sermons almost anywhere will illustrate how frequently he quoted the Scriptures on almost every page. For analysis, six sermons have been selected, one from each of the six decades, 1730's to 1780's.

On January 1st 1733, at St Mary's, Oxford, Wesley preached one of his University sermons, *The Circumcision of the Heart*. It contains one hundred and nineteen biblical quotations; that is, it uses the exact words of the biblical text, from both Testaments, one hundred and nineteen times. The 1746 sermon, *The Way to the Kingdom,* has one hundred biblical quotations and the 1750 discourse, *The Sermon on the Mount XIII*, contains one hundred and one scriptural citations. The sermon entitled, *The Use of Money,* (1760) uses forty nine biblical quotations; *National Sins and Miseries,* (1775), has thirty eight quotations from Scripture, and the 1783 sermon, *The Mystery of Iniquity*, makes use of one hundred scriptural citations. These sermons deal with biblical theology, ethical matters and the 1775 sermon is on a topical subject. While it is very clear that Wesley make more use of

---

[56] John Wesley, *Works [BE]*, Vol. 3, p.122

Scripture in sermons dealing with biblical interpretation than when expanding on ethical or topical matters, yet the use of quoted Scripture texts in all the sermons is very impressive. The figures given for these six sermons have to do with the number of Scripture passages that are quoted verbatim; that is, passages that can be written with quotation marks. In addition, these, and the rest of John Wesley's published sermons, contain also many clear allusions to Scripture passages that are not given in quotation fashion. Altogether the use of Scripture in John Wesley's sermons, both by direct quotation and general reference, is very marked. In a letter to John Newton, Wesley made plain his predilection for the scriptural language. 'The Bible is my standard of *language* as well as sentiment. I endeavour not only to think but to speak *as the oracles of God*...I keep to my old way, and speak neither better nor worse than the Bible.[57] His sermons clearly illustrate that he practised this claim of speaking 'as the oracles of God.'

Wesley's method of introducing the biblical text is also illustrative of how he believed all Scripture to be God's word. Quotations are frequently introduced by phrases such as, 'Thus saith his word,' 'the Lord himself saith,' 'the Lord declared by David,' 'what saith the Holy Ghost?', 'the express declaration of our Lord.' And such like. On other occasions the writer is identified and his words are accepted as God's; 'as the psalmist observes,' 'saith the prophet,' 'the apostle here directly affirms,' 'St Paul informs us,' 'St Peter wrote,' 'as St James saith,' etc. Yet other quotations are used by introductions such as, 'the scripture saith,' 'the scripture avers,' 'thus saith the scripture,' 'let scripture speak.'[58] Both the multiplicity of the biblical texts in Wesley's sermons and the way they are cited and used for illustration, argument and persuasion reveal his deep conviction that they really are 'the oracles of God.'

---

[57] John Wesley, *Letters*, Vol. 5, p.8.

[58] It should also be noted that in Wesley's sermons a majority of the Scripture citations are quoted without any kind of introduction. Wesley weaves the exact words of the biblical text into his own sentence and usually indicates these by using quotation marks.

It is not only in his sermons, however, that John Wesley demonstrates his wholehearted allegiance to the supreme authority of Holy Scripture. His other writings are likewise replete with the words and doctrines of the Bible. From the year 1739, when his 'field-preaching' ministry began in Bristol, he commenced a half-century of writing in connection with the Methodist movement. These writings included letters, treatises, apologias, grammars, compilations and extracts from other writers, the fifty volumes of the, *Christian Library,* and the, *Explanatory Notes,* on both the Old and New Testaments. All these writings that are original to Wesley, that is, the letters, treatises and apologias, are characterised by his fondness for quoting Scripture. Whether he was arguing for the fundamental doctrines of the historic Christian faith, answering attacks made on Methodism by clerical opponents like Bishop Lavington, dealing with a difficulty in one of the circuits or advising one of his followers on spiritual matters, Wesley quoted the Scriptures in support of all his arguments.

This is amply illustrated by looking at his 1743 publication, *An Earnest Appeal to men of Reason and Religion,* and his 1745 follow-up, *A Farther Appeal....*, aimed at self-assured 'men of reason' who felt no need of the Christian revelation, and 'men of religion' whose formal orthodoxy fell short of saving faith, Wesley set out to explain and defend scriptural Christianity in general and 'Methodism' in particular. Arguments drawn from the Christian tradition, especially the Anglican tradition, are common throughout the two works. There are constant references to, and citations from, the, *Book of Common Prayer*, the, *Homilies,* and the, *Thirty-Nine Articles*, for John Wesley held a life-long tradition that the Church of England was 'the most scriptural national Church in the world.'[59] From the early centuries of the Church Ignatius, Chrysostom and Augustine are quoted, and the, *Constitutions and Canons Ecclesiastical*, George Herbert, and Bishops Edmund Bonner, John Pearson, Richard Smalbroke and George Berkeley are among the Anglican representatives. But while these voices of the Christian tradition, past and present, speak loudly, Wesley argues, in

[59] John Wesley, *Works*, Vol. 13, p.272.

his defence, it is thc voice of God in Holy Scripture that speaks first, last and loudest in these two apologias. In the opening paragraph of, *An Earnest Appeal*, there are three Scripture quotations, and the fifty-six Scripture quotations that appear in the first ten pages illustrate John Wesley's constant appeal to the authority of Scripture. It is not merely, however, the plethora of Biblical citations in these two works that indicate Wesley's appeal to the Scripture. The whole argument is based on the supposition that the Christian faith, as represented by the official teaching of the Church of England, and now being revived by 'Methodism' throughout the country, is supported by the bedrock of Holy Scripture.

One other area of John Wesley's use of Scripture needs to be noted briefly. This has to do with the daily devotional reading of the Bible as he practised it and recommended it to his people. In the 'Preface' to the published sermons where he described himself as 'a man of one book,' there is a passage of simple, beautiful English prose where he lays before us his method of Bible study.

> Here then, I am, far from the busy ways of men. I sit down alone: only God is here. In his presence I open, I read his Book; for this end, to find the way to heaven. Is there a doubt concerning the meaning of what I read? Does anything appear dark or intricate? I lift up my heart to the Father of lights: 'Lord, is it not thy Word, "If any man lack wisdom, let him ask of God?"... Thou hast said, "if any man be willing to do thy will, he shall know." I am willing to do, let me know thy will.'[60]

When he published his, *Explanatory Notes on the Old Testament,* in 1765 he prefaced them with directions on the best way to study the Bible.

> If you desire to read the Scriptures in such a manner as may most effectually answer this end (to understand the things of God), would it not be advisable (1) To set apart a little time, if you can, every morning and evening for this purpose? (2) At each time, if you have leisure, to read a chapter out of the Old,

---

[60] John Wesley, *Works [BE]*, Vol. 1, pp.105,106.

> and one out of the New Testament; if you cannot do this, to take a single chapter, or a part of one? (3) To read this with a single eye to know the whole will of God, and a fixed resolution to do it?[61]

Although John Wesley did not give much attention to theories on the nature of biblical inspiration, he was sure that the devout study of Scripture was accompanied by divine help. When he wrote his, *Explanatory Notes,* on 2 Tim. 3:16, 'All scripture is inspired of God,' he avowed: 'The Spirit not only once inspired those who wrote it, but continually inspires, supernaturally assists those who read it with earnest prayer.'

John Wesley's Principles of Interpretation

With this evidence of how John Wesley was convinced that Holy Scripture was 'the oracles of God,' and further evidence of how he used it as fully and finally authoritative in theological construction and pastoral counsel, it is time to look at his principles of interpretation. How did he interpret the text of Scripture? The answer to this hermeneutical question cannot be found in any single passage from his voluminous writings. It must be deduced from a careful study of his use of the Scripture text in his many biblical, theological and pastoral writings and publications. Three fairly clear principles of interpretation emerge from this study.

First, *the literal sense of the text is primary*. John Wesley believed that the English Bible current in his day was a completely reliable translation of the original Biblical manuscripts. This meant that the average man and woman who could read the Bible, without the benefit of knowledge of the original languages and without recourse to learned commentaries, yet had in their grasp God's saving Word. God had given his Word in order that sinners might find eternal life and that believers might be built up in faith and holiness. To that end, Scripture carried its meaning plainly in the text. As early as 1727 Wesley was

[61] John Wesley, *Explanatory Notes upon the Old Testament*, Edinburgh, 1765, p.ix.

convinced of this canon of interpretation. In an Epworth sermon he declared that the true preacher explains the text 'in the most natural, obvious way, by what precedes and what follows the place in question.'[62]

Early as 1738 he replied to an enquiry about what the principles of this new sect of 'Methodists' were. 'I answer clearly: We have no principles, but those revealed in the Word of God; in the interpretation whereof we always judge the most literal sense to be the best, unless where the literal sense of one contradicts some other scripture.'[63] Years later he gave similar advice to one of his young preachers, Samuel Furley. 'The general rule of interpreting Scripture is this: the literal sense of every text is to be taken, if it be not contrary to some other texts.'[64] In instances where the literal sense did seem to be in conflict with other texts, then the text being considered must be compared with other Scripture texts whose meaning is clear. Wesley was convinced that in Scripture the vast majority of its texts carried 'a plain, obvious sense.' In two sermons on, *The Witness of the Spirit*, he expounded at some length on Rom. 8:16, 'The Spirit itself beareth witness with our spirit that we are the children of God.' Arguing that there is agreement among Christians that 'the fruit of the Spirit' is evidence of the Spirit's work within, Wesley goes further. 'The point in question is whether there be any direct testimony of the Spirit at all.' In other words, does Paul mean that the Christian can enjoy an 'inner expression of the soul' by which he knows 'immediately and directly' that he is 'a child of God'? Wesley's answer is unequivocal. 'I believe there is, because that is the plain, natural meaning of the text.'[65]

This advocacy of the literal meaning of the text did not mean, however, that John Wesley merely took the words of the English Bible, selected them at random and pasted them together as a kind of proof-text collage. In preparation for his, *Explanatory Notes on the New*

---

[62] John Wesley, *Works [BE]*, Vol. 4, p.249.
[63] John Wesley, *Letters*, Vol. 1, p.234.
[64] John Wesley, *Letters*, Vol. 3, p.129.
[65] John Wesley, *Works [BE]*, Vol. 1, p.288.

Testament, he made it clear in the 'Preface' that while the exposition would be based on the current King James text, in significant places he was departing from it. These departures were in those passages where the English translation can be brought 'nearer to the original.' Likewise the Greek texts that lie behind the common translation are not always the 'most correct.' With this proposal to test the Authorised text by the best-available Greek texts, Wesley prepared the English text for his *Notes*. While in the main it followed the King James text, yet in many passages it departed from it – and the departures can be traced to the instances where Wesley believed that there were Greek texts with readings superior to those of the, *Textus Receptus*. Wesley claimed in the 'Preface' that he wrote for 'plain, unlettered men, who understand only their mother tongue, and yet reverence and love the word of God, and have a desire to save their souls.' That did not mean, however, that Wesley was content to use the common English text, and the Greek behind it, uncritically. These were the oracles of God and in order to help those who sought to save their souls, Wesley felt bound to search out the best-available Greek text.

In a majority of the places where Wesley departed from the common English text, his preferred text anticipates the work of the Oxford and Cambridge revisers of one hundred and thirty years later. This can be seen by comparing the text in Wesley's, *Explanatory Notes on the New Testament,* with the text of the 1880, *Revised Version,* New Testament. This comparison does not suggest that the committee of scholars appointed by the Convocation of Canterbury in 1870 consulted Wesley's New Testament, but it does argue that John Wesley, working alone in the early 1750's, came to conclusions about the relative value of Greek manuscripts that were confirmed by these scholars in the next century.

John Wesley's second canon of interpretation was that Scripture *is its own best interpreter*. Arising from his conviction that all Scripture was the oracles of God, Wesley was sure that all of this divine revelation was a unity, any one part agreeing and confirming the other parts. In the 'Preface' to his published sermons in 1746 he spoke of his own method of understanding the biblical text as searching after and considering 'parallel passages of Scripture, comparing spiritual things with spiritual.'[66] Earlier, when the Moravian, Peter Bohler, was discussing the nature of saving faith, Wesley was sure that the Bible contradicted Bohler's doctrine. 'I first consulted the Scripture. But when I set aside the glosses of men, and simply considered the words of God, comparing them together and endeavouring to illustrate the obscure by the plainer passages, I found they all made against me, and was forced to retreat.'[67] The reference here to the recognition that the plainer parts of Scripture 'illustrate the obscure,' indicate that Wesley not only held this canon of interpretation as early as 1738 but he was willing to abide by it when being forced to admit that he held an inadequate view of saving faith. Wesley often made use of this canon by phrases like 'the whole scripture,' 'all the scriptures,' 'innumerable scriptures,' 'the whole tenor of scripture,' 'the general tenor of scripture,' 'the whole Christian revelation. This meant that any interpretation of a particular passage of Scripture seems to teach a truth out of harmony with the rest of Scripture, then we can be sure that our interpretation of that one passage is false. Wesley made particular use of this canon in some of his polemic writings. In his sermon, *Free Grace*, he objected to any passage of Scripture that was brought forward to prove the doctrine of reprobation, viz. That God had condemned some men and women to eternal damnation by an inscrutable decree. Wesley argued that it was preferable to confess that the true meaning of some Scripture passages is beyond our present knowledge rather than give them a meaning which contradicted the rest of Scripture. So convinced was he that Scripture did not teach a doctrine of reprobation, he flatly refused any Scripture advanced for that purpose.

> Whatever that Scripture proves, it can never prove this. Whatever its true meaning be, this cannot be its true meaning. It cannot mean, whatever it mean besides, that the God of truth is a liar. Let it mean what it will, it cannot mean that the Judge of

---

[66] John Wesley, *Works [BE]*, Vol. 1, p.106.
[67] John Wesley, *Works [BE]*, Vol. 18, p.248.

> all the world is unjust. No Scripture can mean that God is not love, or that his mercy is not over all his works.[68]

In a later polemic on the same subject, Wesley was still asserting that any passage allegedly used to prove reprobation would contradict the plain teaching of all the Scriptures.

> This is my grand objection to the doctrine of unconditional election. That it is an error, I know; because, if this were true, the whole Scripture must be false... Reprobation I can never agree to while I believe the Scripture to be of God, as being utterly irreconcilable to the whole scope and tenor both of the Old and New Testament.[69]

In asserting that Scripture is its own best interpreter, Wesley was in line with an accepted canon of Reformation exegesis. Arthur Skevington Wood has demonstrated that Martin Luther followed this approach when he dealt with the Biblical text and especially in answering his critics. 'That is the true method of interpretation,' says Luther, which puts Scripture alongside Scripture in a right and proper way... Scripture is its own light. It is a fine thing when Scripture explains itself.'[70] When John Wesley set out to show that ordinary Christians could understand the Bible without having to defer to the Church of Rome's claim to be the sole interpreter of Scripture, he argued Scripture's supremacy over all ecclesiastical traditions. 'In all cases, the Church is to be judged by the Scriptures, not the Scripture by the Church. And Scripture is the best expounder of Scripture. The best way, therefore, to understand it, is carefully to compare Scripture with Scripture, and thereby learn the true meaning of it.'[71]

An important element in this canon was how Wesley understood the commandments of God as 'covered promises.' This arose from the correlation he perceived between the law and the gospel in Christian

---

[68] John Wesley, *Works [BE]*, Vol. 3, p.556.

[69] John Wesley, *Works*, Vol. 10, pp.256.

[70] 'Luther's Principles of Biblical Interpretation,' *Travelling Man*, P. Taylor and H Mellor, Ilkeston, 1994, p.97.

[71] John Wesley, *Works*, Vol. 10, p.142.

experience. In a letter to a Methodist layman, Wesley complained that a 'new style' gospel preaching was being promoted in many of the circuits. It concentrated solely on the Christian's privileges in Christ but was careful to say nothing about the Christian's responsibility. Wesley censured it as offering nothing but 'cordials, cordials,' and warned that it opened the door to Antinomianism.[72] He had spelt out the law/gospel relationship in Discourse V of his, *Sermon on the Mount*. Based on Matthew 5:17-20, it set out to explain the words of Jesus. 'Think not that I am come to destroy the law and the prophets: I am not come to destroy, but to fulfil.' This means, Wesley argued, that there is no contrariety between law and gospel. This means in Christian experience that poverty of spirit, purity of heart and whatever else the holy law of God enjoins, are but great and precious when seen in gospel light.

> There is therefore the closest connection that can be conceived between the law and the gospel. On the one hand the law continually makes way for and points us to the gospel; on the other the gospel continually leads us to a more exact fulfilling of the law. The law, for instance, requires us to love God, to love our neighbour.... We feel we are not sufficient for these things.... But we see a promise of God to give us that love, and to make us humble, meek and holy. We lay hold of this gospel.... and 'the righteousness of the law is fulfilled in us' through faith.
>
> We may yet farther observe that every command in Holy Writ is only a covered promise.... God hath engaged to give whatever he commands. Does he command us.... 'to be holy as he is holy'? It is enough. He will work in us this very thing. It shall be unto us according to his word.[73]

This understanding of the commandments as 'covered promises' became very important for John Wesley in his explication of the doctrine of Christian holiness. He had long been convinced that preaching justification by faith (that is, what Christ has done *for* us) without the corollary doctrine of sanctification by faith (that is, what

---

72 John Wesley, Letters, Vol. 3, pp.78-85.

73 John Wesley, *Works [BE]*, Vol. 1, pp.554, 555.

Christ wants to do *in* us) was tantamount to promoting Antinomianism. Many contemporary evangelicals repudiated Wesley's doctrine of Christian holiness as a return to legalism and denial of gospel privileges. Wesley stoutly answered no. God commands his people to be holy because, in Christ, he has already made provision for their holiness. He gave pointed emphasis to this law/gospel command and provision in his 1784 sermon, 'On Perfection.'

> That general and unlimited promise... 'I will put my laws in their mind, and write them in their hearts,' turns all the commands into promises... The command is equivalent to a promise, and gives us full reason to expect that he will work in us what he requires of us... The command of God given by St Peter, 'Be ye holy, as he that hath called you is holy,' implies a promise that we shall be thus holy if we are not wanting to ourselves. Nothing can be wanting on God's part. As he has called us to holiness he is undoubtedly willing, as well as able, to work his holiness in us. For he cannot mock his helpless creatures, calling us to receive what he never intends to give.[74]

John Wesley's third principle of interpretation was a soteriological consideration designated by him 'the analogy of faith.' The phrase was not original with him for it had been in use in Protestant exegesis in England for more than a century since the Reformation. Gerald Bray has shown that the central issue of contention between Protestant and Catholic scholars was whether the Bible was self-interpreting, as the Protestant claimed, or needed the authority of the church, as the Catholics claimed. The principle of self-interpretation meant that the Bible was clear in its meaning and therefore it should be interpreted in a literal sense. 'Those parts of the Bible which were not clear were to be interpreted by the analogy of faith. This meant that whatever was said about them should be in agreement with what the clearer parts of Scripture already made plain, and that nothing should be inferred from an unclear passage which could not be proved from another, more obvious, text.'[75]

---

[74] John Wesley, *Works [BE]*, Vol. 3, p.77.

[75] Gerald Bray, *Biblical Interpretation: Past and Present*, pp.192, 193.

The first mention of 'the analogy of faith' in the Wesley corpus is in a letter to John from his mother Susanna in 1725. John had written to her, confessing his problem with Article XVII dealing with predestination. Susanna replied by defining predestination in terms of God's foreknowledge, and then he added: 'This is the sum of what I believe concerning predestination, which I think is agreeable to the analogy of faith, since it never derogates from God's free grace, nor impairs the liberty of man.'[76] Clearly Susanna means that her interpretation of the doctrine of predestination is in harmony with the rest of Scripture. A year later, in his Oxford sermon, *On Guardian Angels*, John Wesley used the same phrase. He argued that it is permissible to enquire about the origin and mission of angels, provided 'we proceed with due reverence and humility, and do not contradict the analogy of our faith,'[77] Wesley next used the words in his 1742 tract, *The Principles of a Methodist*.' Using a catena of Scripture quotes to describe what a 'Methodist' is, he asked if there was anything in this portrayal that was not consistent with Scripture or that was contrary to 'the analogy of faith.'[78] Four years later he opined that many notions about the doctrine of justification by faith were inconsistent with 'the whole analogy of faith.'[79] In all these instances Wesley uses the words 'the analogy of faith' to mean 'the general sense of the Scriptures.'

It was in his, *Explanatory Notes,* on Romans, published in 1755, that Wesley used this phrase to mean more than just the general tenor of Scripture. In Rom. 12:6 where the AV text reads, 'Having then gifts differing.... let us prophesy according to the proportion of faith,' Wesley translated, ... 'let us prophesy according to the analogy of faith.' While that clearly means 'in harmony with the rest of Scripture,' Wesley makes it mean significantly more.

> St. Peter expresses it as, 'As the oracles of God' – according to their general tenor; according to that grand scheme of doctrine

---

[76] John Wesley, *Works [BE],* Vol. 25, p.180.
[77] John Wesley, *Works [BE]*, Vol. 4, p.231.
[78] John Wesley, *Works [BE]*, Vol. 9, p.55.
[79] John Wesley, *Works [BE]*, Vol. 1, p.183.

> delivered therein, touching original sin, justification by faith, etc. There is a wonderful analogy between all these: and a close connection between the chief heads of that 'faith which was once delivered to the saints.'[80]

Now 'the analogy of faith' has reference specifically to the fundamental doctrines of Scripture, including original sin and justification by faith. When he published his, *Explanatory Notes on the Old Testament,* a decade later, the concept of the 'analogy' was more developed. Advising his readers on the best way to study the Scriptures he wrote: 'Have a constant eye to the analogy of faith, the connection and harmony there is between those grand fundamental doctrines, original sin, justification by faith, the new birth, inward and outward holiness.'[81] Four years earlier he had attempted, unsuccessfully to bring about a kind of fraternal union among the evangelical clergy, those whom he described as preaching the three grand scriptural doctrines – original Sin, Justification by Faith, and Holiness consequent thereon. John Wesley was clearly maintaining that all the teachings and doctrines of the Bible can be reduced to three that incorporate all the rest – the grand fundamental doctrines of original sin, justification by faith and holiness of heart and life. By equating the analogy of faith with these three doctrines, he was establishing by it a hermeneutical principle significantly different from how it had been used by Reformation and Puritan scholars. While they employed it to mean the general harmony found in all the Scriptures, Wesley deliberately turned it into a soteriological principle. All Scripture, he maintained, must be read and understood in the light of its *saving* purpose. Sin, grace and holiness comprehend the totality of Scripture teaching. Wesley is adamant that the meaning of every single passage of Scripture, in both Testaments, is ultimately understood in the light of these three doctrines.

In the interpretation of Scripture John Wesley freely employed and constantly commended to others the invaluable help given by tradition,

---

[80] John Wesley, St. Paul Epistle to the Romans, 12:6.

[81] John Wesley, *Explanatory Notes upon the Old Testament, Preface,* p.ix.

reason and experience. In half a century of preaching and theological construction, he certainly worked with what the late Albert Outler designated as Wesley's quadrilateral; Scripture, tradition, reason and experience. By tradition Wesley meant the accumulated wisdom provided by the Church's Fathers, scholars and theologians in every age. By reason he meant the necessary discipline of subjecting all data, Scriptural and non-Scriptural, to the test of common sense. Believing passionately that God can be known by men and women in their own spirits – the religion of the heart – he argued that experience can confirm the experiential truths taught in the Bible. But Scripture is the word of God and no matter what interpretative help comes from tradition, reason and experience, Scripture alone is 'the oracles of God.' In a lifetime of preaching, travelling, writing and organising the Methodist revival, John Wesley's main business was helping others to find what he himself had found – the way to heaven. In every respect he embodied his autobiographical description – a man of one Book.

Lecture 2
JOHN WESLEY AND SALVATION

Throughout almost his entire ministry and certainly post the heart-warming of May 1738, John Wesley's most pressing concern was with the doctrine of salvation. How men and women are reconciled to God, confirmed of their acceptance in Christ and built up in holy faith dominated his life's work for more than fifty years. Returning to England from Georgia early in 1738, Wesley expressed this concern in an autobiographical memorandum. 'I want that faith which none can have without knowing that he hath it...for whosoever hath it.... is freed from sin.'[82] When he published the first edition of his sermons in 1746, the soteriological concern for himself and others was still uppermost in his mind. 'I want to know one thing, the way to heaven.'[83] In 1738 he had made the great personal discovery that the way to heaven was through justification by faith. At the very end of his life, when, in his own words, he was 'on the borders of the grave,' he confessed: 'About fifty years ago I had a clearer view than before of justification by faith. In this, from that very hour, I never varied, not a hair's breadth.... By the grace of God I still witness the same confession, "By grace ye are saved through faith."'[84]

The previous Lecture dealt, in summary, with John Wesley's understanding of original sin and prevenient grace. He believed that the Holy Spirit worked on the consciences of sinners to awaken them to an understanding of their sinful condition. How, then, does the sinner come to the place of reconciliation before God? What is the process that brings the awakened sinner from condemnation to forgiveness?, from alienation to the kingdom of God? The answers to these questions lie in Wesley's understanding of the doctrine of salvation. This Lecture will examine how he understood salvation. In its full extent, it is the whole work of God in the soul from the first

---

[82] John Wesley, *Works [BE]*, Vol. 18, p.216.
[83] John Wesley, Preface, *Works [BE]*, Vol. 1, p.105.
[84] John Wesley, *Works [BE]*, Vol. 4, pp.147, 148.

dawning of prevenient grace until resurrection glory. In his 1745, *Farther Appeal*, Wesley gave a very concise definition of what he meant by this term.

> By salvation I mean, not barely (according to the vulgar notion) deliverance from hell, or going to heaven, but a present deliverance from sin, a restoration of the soul to its primitive health, its original purity; a recovery of the divine nature; the renewal of our souls after the image of God in righteousness and true holiness, in justice, mercy and truth. This implies all holy and heavenly tempers, and by consequence all holiness of conversation.[85]

When Wesley commonly spoke about salvation he was usually referring to the doctrines of justification and sanctification. He defined these terms very carefully and the relationship between them. 'The two grand branches' of 'the proper Christian salvation' are 'justification and sanctification.' By the former we are saved from the guilt of sin and restored to God's image.[86]

Eighteen days after his Aldersgate 'heart-warming' experience, John Wesley preached in St Mary's, Oxford. This was his tenth university sermon and in tone and intention it was markedly different from the earlier extant sermons. Based on Eph. 2:8, 'By grace ye are saved through faith,' Wesley entitled it, *Salvation by Faith*. In all his subsequent editions of published sermons it was always sermon number one. It brought together the various elements that had influenced Wesley's soteriological thinking so deeply in the preceding years; Scripture, the Anglican Homilies and the Moravian emphasis on faith as trust in Christ crucified.

Defining saving faith, Wesley argued it is not the faith of heathens who believe that God exists. Neither is it the faith of devils that believe in God and his Son whom he has sent, for while they believe this and tremble, they do not repent. Neither is saving faith the kind of faith the

---

[85] John Wesley, *Works [BE]*, Vol. 11, p.106.
[86] John Wesley, *Works [BE]*, Vol. 3, p.204.

disciples had while Jesus was on earth, for that faith did not yet comprehend the significance of his death and resurrection. Then Wesley gave his careful definition of the faith by which we are saved.

> Christian faith is not only a full reliance on the blood of Christ, a trust in the merits of his life, death and resurrection, a recumbency upon him as our atonement and our life, as given for us, and living in us. It is a sure confidence which a man hath in God, that through the merits of Christ his sins are forgiven, and he reconciled to the favour of God. [87]

This definition clearly reflects the Anglican Homily entitled 'Of Salvation.' But this definition just as clearly has echoes of the Moravian understanding of saving faith to which Wesley had been exposed for the past three years. In particular the emphasis on the death of Christ, with references to 'the blood of Christ' and 'him as our atonement and our life,' is very much in the Moravian strain.

Having defined saving faith, Wesley then proceeded to delineate what he meant by 'salvation.' It is a present salvation by which the penitent believer is saved from sin. The guilt of past sins is cancelled and the Christian is saved from the fear of damnation and from the power of wilful sinning. This salvation is further defined as 'justification,' and to be justified is to be 'saved by faith,' it is to be 'born again,' it is to be 'born of the Spirit.' From this understanding of salvation by faith John Wesley did not depart for the rest of his life. This Oxford sermon was indeed, in Albert Outler's words, 'a positive evangelical manifesto.'[88] It was this understanding of saving faith and a present salvation from sin that would constitute the heart of John Wesley's evangel as he led the work of the revival. There were some later and very important nuances that emerged in Wesley's thinking about salvation, but this Oxford proclamation of salvation by faith would remain the bedrock of all his preaching and theological construction.

---

[87] John Wesley, *Works [BE]*, Vol. 1, p.121.

[88] Albert Outler, First Four Sermons, *Works* [BE], Vol. 1, p.110.

In this sermon Wesley spoke of salvation by faith as being expressed by the word 'justification.' This term emerged as central to his understanding of the gospel and all his later writings are replete with mentions of it. His insistence on its importance also reflects his own spiritual pilgrimage. In the weeks leading up to May 24, 1738, he wrote to his former mentor, William Law, and strongly reproved him for not clearly enunciating justification by faith. By this date Wesley was convinced that the root problem of his Oxford 'Holy Club' experience was that he was vainly seeking sanctification without the needed foundation of justification through faith. Somewhat rashly he laid all the blame at Law's door. He alleged that he had been diligently following the directions laid down in Law's two treatises, *Christian Perfection,* and, *Serious Call*. But this counsel brought no relief and Wesley declared that if he had not received help from another quarter, he would have 'groaned till death' under this 'heavy yoke.' Why, demanded Wesley, 'did I scarce ever hear you name the name of Christ?' Why had Law not directed him to faith in Christ's atonement? 'What must I do to be saved?' Then Wesley spoke directly to the man he once characterised as the 'father of the Holy Club.' 'I beseech you, sir, by the mercies of God, to consider deeply and impartially whether the reason of your never pressing this upon me was not this, that you had it not yourself?'[89] Whatever may be thought of this egregious attack on William Law, it is clear that John Wesley believed that until early in 1738, he had been confused and misled about the meaning and priority of justification by faith. Oxford Methodism, in Wesley's opinion, had failed to discover this vital Christian doctrine and it is hardly incidental that the first Oxford sermon following the Moravian 'heart-warming,' concentrated on salvation by faith.

Another of Wesley's early landmark sermons was 'Justification by Faith,' published in the first series of his, *Sermons on Several Occasions*. He based it on Rom. 4:5, 'To him that worketh not, but believeth on him that justifieth the ungodly, his faith is counted to him for righteousness.' Although the publication date is 1746, Wesley

---

[89] John Wesley, *The Letters of John Wesley*, Vol. 1, pp. 238-240.

preached on this text only four days after his Aldersgate experience and on many occasions in the next few years. This sermon dealt with the same biblical doctrines expressed in 'Salvation by faith' but the explication of the various theological concepts is fuller and more definitive. Every subsequent sermon that Wesley preached and published on justification can be measured by this sermon, well described by Albert Outler as 'the earliest full summary of Wesley's soteriology in the basic form in which it will continue.'[90]

How sinners are justified before God is a question of the greatest moment. The sermon's opening paragraphs summarise Wesley's understanding of man's creation in primitive holiness, his probation and fall in Eden and how by that 'one man sin entered into the world.' In the fullness of time a second representative of mankind came into the world who 'tasted death for every man.' By this atonement God has now reconciled the world to himself, and, for the sake of his Son, to remit the due condemnation of sinners and restore them to spiritual life as the guarantee of life eternal. This, says Wesley, is the whole doctrine of justification. By the sacrifice of the second Adam, the representative of us all, there is no condemnation for those who are 'justified freely by his grace through the redemption that is in Christ Jesus' (Rom. 3:24). What does it mean, then, to be justified? In his usual style, Wesley answers this question by telling us first what it is not. It is not sanctification for that means being made actually just and righteous, and although sanctification is the immediate consequence of justification, it is yet a distinct gift of God. The former means what God does *for us* through his Son, while the latter means what he *works in us* by his Spirit. Neither does justification mean being cleared from the accusations made either by the devil, 'the accuser of the brethren,' or by the law. Nor does justification mean that God attributes to sinners a righteousness, which in fact they do not have. Wesley's target here is an over-emphasis on a forensic interpretation of justification by which Christ's righteousness is imputed to the sinner's credit. God can never declare that we are righteous or holy just because his Son is holy.

---

[90] John Wesley, *Works [BE]*, Vol. 1, p.182.

'He can no more in this manner confound me with Christ than with David or Abraham.'[91]

Having cleared the way to speak positively about justification, Wesley moved on to a definition. 'The plain scriptural notion of justification is pardon, the forgiveness of sins. It is that act of God the Father whereby, for the sake of the propitiation made by the blood of his Son, he "showeth forth his righteousness by the remission of the sins that are past."'[92] This was intended to be a formal, theological definition of justification and it is surely significant that nothing like it appears in John Wesley's writings prior to 1738. That it was in that momentous year he came to this understanding is not only clearly evidenced by his general soteriological writings subsequent to 1738, but also by his express references. Defending himself against the cavils of Dr. John Erskine in April 1765, he wrote: 'In the main point, Justification by Faith, I have not wavered a moment for these seven and twenty years,' a reference to 1738.[93] Three weeks later he wrote to John Newton. 'I think on Justification just as I have done any time these seven and twenty years, and just as Mr. Calvin does. In this respect I do not differ from him an hair's breadth.'[94] In these letters John Wesley is not only confirming his affirmation of the doctrine of justification by faith but also drawing attention quite deliberately to 1738 as the year in which that affirmation commenced.

In this sermon Wesley stressed the aspect of forgiveness. Here, as in all his writings, he demonstrates that remarkable facility of quoting appropriate Scripture references, sometimes in full and sometimes partly. The justified person is the one to whom the Lord does not 'impute sin.' He is the man or woman who 'iniquities are forgiven, and whose sins are pardoned.' He will not be condemned, either in this world or the next. His sins, all his past sins, 'in thought, word and deed, "are covered," are blotted out and shall not be remembered against him

---

[91] John Wesley, *Works [BE],* Vol. 1, p.188.
[92] John Wesley, *Works [BE],* Vol. 1, p.189.
[93] John Wesley, *Letters*, Vol. 4, p.295.
[94] John Wesley, *Letters*, Vol. 4, p.298.

anymore.' 'From the time the justified are "accepted through the Beloved, reconciled to God through his blood," he loves and blesses and watches over us for good, even if we had never sinned.'[95]

Then Wesley answered the question – who are they who are justified? The answer is, in the words of the sermon's text, "the ungodly." Sin alone admits of being pardoned; it is our 'righteousness' to which the pardoning God is merciful; it is our 'iniquity' which he remembers no more. This is Wesley's preface to what might be called a not-too-well-disguised attack on the 'holy living' tradition in Anglicanism, a tradition he had fervently embraced in his earlier years. The interpretation of justification he has just evinced, he complains, has not been understood at all by those who assert that a man must be sanctified before he is justified. These theologians, Wesley affirmed, declare that 'universal holiness or obedience must precede justification.' But unless this refers to the justification of believers at the last day, it flatly contradicts what Paul is teaching in Romans 3 and 4. It is not only a contradiction of Paul's teaching, it is 'grossly, intrinsically absurd,' for it is not a saint who is forgiven but a sinner. God does not justify the godly but the ungodly; not those who are holy already but the unholy. The good Shepherd does not only seek and save those already found; he seeks and saves what is lost. He pardons those who need his pardoning love and he saves from guilt sinners of every kind. Not only is Wesley here maintaining his doctrine of justification by faith against those whom he believes have inverted the biblical order of justification and sanctification, but he is equally adamant in maintaining his doctrine of universal sinfulness and the utter helplessness of sinners apart from grace.

Wesley knew that this espousal of justification by works would be objected to by those who maintained that it left no place for good works. Surely, the objection ran, a sinner should feed the hungry and clothe the naked and perform other good works before he is justified? Yes, answered Wesley, he *may* do such good works, and they are good

---

[95] John Wesley, *Works [BE],* Vol. 1, pp.189, 190.

because they are profitable to his fellow men. They will, not, however, bring the sinner to justification or occasion his acceptance before God. In proof of this Wesley quoted from Article XII and XIII of the, *Thirty-Nine Articles*. 'Good works, which are the fruits of faith, follow after justification,' and 'works done before the grace of Christ.... Are not pleasant to God, inasmuch as they spring not from faith in Jesus Christ.'[96] This correlation of saving faith and good works would become a critical point in the development of John Wesley's doctrines in later years, and the strong assertion that good works or holy living are neither possible or demanded prior to justification, would become an important starting point in that controversy. Just as Wesley, in the years immediately following 1738, was absolutely convinced that justification does not flow from good works, so in later years he would be absolutely convinced that good works flow *from* justification.

The sermon then proceeded to examine the grounds of justification; *how* are sinners justified? Wesley answered again in the words of the text – faith. The justified are those who 'believe in him who justifies the ungodly.' God has set forth his Son to be 'a propitiation through faith in his blood.' In that way God is just and 'the justifier of him which believeth in Jesus.' All this means, Wesley argued, that we can conclude, with Paul, that sinners are justified 'by faith without the deeds of the law,' that is, without previous obedience to God's moral law.

What, then, is this faith by which we are justified? Perhaps there is no single definition or description of God's way of salvation in John Wesley's writings more important than this one. For Wesley, true Christian faith has a two-fold significance. First, in general, it is a divine, supernatural conviction of unseen spiritual realities. By using the adjectives 'divine' and 'supernatural,' Wesley means that this certainty does not arise within us merely by the exercise of our own intuitive spiritual senses. Rather, this kind of faith is the gift of God, and is directly the consequence of prevenient grace. This general

---

[96] Articles of Religion XII, 'Of Good Works:' XIII 'Of Works before Justification.'

understanding of faith goes as far as believing the doctrine of Christ's incarnation and atonement. But it also goes further because it embraces the understanding not only that God in Christ died for the sins of the world, but, says Wesley, that 'he died for *my* sins, that he loved *me*, and gave himself for *me*.' Wesley is sure that he cannot define this justifying faith better than is done in the *Homilies*. 'The only instrument of salvation is faith; that is, a sure trust and confidence that God both hath and will forgive our sins, that he hath accepted us into his favour, for the merits of Christ's death and passion.'[97] This careful use of Scripture, illustrated by the formularies of the Church of England, enabled Wesley to lay down a soteriological foundation on which he could base his whole theological system and his preaching ministry. 'At what time soever a sinner thus believes, be it in early childhood, in the strength of his years, or when he is old and hoary-headed, God justifieth that ungodly one; God for the sake of his Son pardoneth and absolveth him who had in him till then no good thing.'[98]

Wesley was insistent that this doctrine of justification by faith must be plainly understood. To that end he reiterated the importance of saving faith by showing that it is the only *necessary* condition of justification. At the very moment that God gives faith (for it is 'the gift of God') to the awakened sinner, in that moment, in Paul's words, his faith is 'counted to him for righteousness.' This is the only condition without which none is justified; 'the only thing that is immediately, indispensably, absolutely requisite in order to pardon.[99] This proposition can be put another way. Supposing it was possible for a sinner to have everything else, yet, without faith, he cannot be justified; likewise, if he lacks everything else but has faith, he cannot but be justified. 'Suppose, I say, this sinner, helpless and hopeless, casts himself wholly on the mercy of God in Christ (which indeed he cannot do but by the grace of God), who can doubt but he is forgiven in that moment?'[100]

---

[97] Second Sermon on the Passion, *Homilies*, pp.382-383, pp 457-8.
[98] Sermon on the Sacraments, First Part, p.399.
[99] John Wesley, *Works [BE]*, Vol. 1, p.196.
[100] John Wesley, *Works [BE]*, Vol. 2, pp.162, 163.

In this very careful enunciation of justification by faith, what is somewhat surprising is the brief mention made of the sinner's need of repentance. In other places, he speaks at large of repentance being that deep consciousness of total inner corruption, of the will being perverse and distorted, of living in spiritual darkness and error and covered with the shadow of death.[101] Here repentance is described 'neither more nor less than a deep sense of the want of all good, and the presence of all evil.' This repentance is spoken of as given by God, by which Wesley seems to mean that the Spirit works such a sense of self-revelation in the sinner's heart that he knows and feels and acknowledges himself to be lost and undone. In that awakened sense of helplessness, that is, of repentance, God gives the gift of faith to believe in Christ. Twenty years later Wesley argued in more detail the relationship between repentance and faith. God commands sinners to repent and 'bring forth fruits meet for repentance.' But Wesley avers that repentance and its fruits are conditionally necessary for justification but faith is 'immediately and directly' necessary to justification. A sinner might have ever so much repentance and even the fruits required for repentance, but all of this is of no avail because he cannot be justified until he believes.[102]

This indispensable condition of faith for justification solves, Wesley believes, the apparent dilemma between God's will and human responsibility in Romans 9. The terms of the sinner's pardon do not rest with man but with God. God says, 'I will have mercy on whom I will have mercy;' namely on him who believes in Jesus. Likewise he 'hardens' whom he will; that is, he leaves to the hardness of their own hearts those who 'believe not.' This condition of humble, penitent, believing faith, also answers the pride natural to sinful man. Pride destroyed the angels and tempted Adam and Eve who were promised they would be 'as gods.' In his infinite wisdom God appointed a condition of reconciliation that humbles the sinner to the dust. He who would be justified must come to God 'as a mere sinner, inwardly and

---

[101] John Wesley, *Works [BE],* Vol. 1, p.196.
[102] John Wesley, *Works [BE],* Vol. 2, pp.162, 163.

outwardly, self-destroyed and self-condemned, bringing nothing to God but ungodliness only, pleading nothing of his own but sin and misery.'[103]

This sermon on justification by faith was, and remained, the clearest exposition of this doctrine in all Wesley's writings. It is important to remember it was a sermon and not just a theological treatise. It was meant first, not for perusal by the curious, but to be heard in the open spaces of Britain by those to whom Wesley believed God sent him and the Methodist preachers. This piece of very practical theology dealt with the fundamental question of the Revival – how are sinners reconciled to God? Wesley's conclusion is a good example of how he must have so often joined Scripture to Scripture as he made an open invitation, in short, pithy, and dramatic sentences, that his hearers would repent and believe this gospel.

> Thou ungodly one who hearest or readest these words, thou, vile, helpless, miserable sinner, I charge thee before God, go straight unto him with all thy ungodliness. Go as altogether ungodly, guilty, lost, destroyed, deserving and dropping into hell.... As such thou shalt be brought unto 'the blood of sprinkling.' Thus 'look unto Jesus.' There is 'the Lamb of God who taketh away thy sins,' Plead thou no works, no righteousness of thine own; no humility, contrition, sincerity. In no wise... No. Plead thou singly the blood of the covenant, the ransom paid for thy proud, stubborn, sinful soul. Who art thou that now seest and feelest both thine inward and outward ungodliness? Thou art the man! I want thee for my Lord. I challenge *thee* for a child of God by faith. The Lord hath need of thee. Thou feelest thou art just fit for hell art just to advance his glory: the glory of his free grace, justifying the ungodly and him that worketh not. O come quickly. Believe in the Lord Jesus; and thou, even thou, art reconciled to God.[104]

This sermon is as clear an example of salvation *sola fidei* as anything found in the writings of Martin Luther or John Calvin. As to its central

[103] John Wesley, *Works [BE],* Vol. 1, p.198.
[104] John Wesley, *Works [BE],* Vol. 1, pp.198, 199.

tenet, viz. that sinners are justified by grace through faith, John Wesley could indeed claim that he varied not a hair's breadth from the teaching of Calvin. Wesley's whole argument has to do with how God saves penitent sinners who have faith in Christ as their Redeemer. It proclaims forgiveness, reconciliation, adoption and the promise of eternal life. What this sermon does not say, nor was it intended to say, is what happens to the sinner who is justified? What change in heart, in intention, in motivation, takes place in the life of the man or woman who is justified? Or is justification merely a forensic transaction, in which the sinner is given a new relationship with God but whose inner condition of sinfulness remains as it was before?

John Wesley gave a very definite answer to these questions – in his understanding of what the New Testament means by the new birth. Throughout his writings no biblical doctrine appears more frequently than that of the new birth, also often referred to as regeneration. Two of Wesley's sermons deal with the new birth in detail; *The Great Privilege of those that are Born of God* and, *The New Birth.* Wesley coupled his understanding of justification with that of spiritual new birth and set them both in their place in the scheme of Christian redemption. He spelt out their relationship to each other and their importance.

> If any doctrine within the whole compass of Christianity may be properly termed fundamental they are doubtless these two – the doctrine of justification, and that of the new birth: the former relating to that great work which God does *for us*, in forgiving our sins; the latter to the great work which God does in us, renewing our fallen nature. In order of time neither of these is before the other. In the moment we are justified by the grace of God through the redemption that is in Jesus we are also 'born of the Spirit;' but in order of thinking, as it is termed, justification precedes the new birth. We first conceive his wrath to be turned away, and then his Spirit to work in our hearts.[105]

[105] John Wesley, *Works [BE],* Vol. 2, p.187.

Wesley was clearly convinced that while sinners are saved by grace alone through faith, that faith is not alone. It is wrought in the heart by the Spirit who begins the great work of transforming the sinner into a saint. Wesley's treatment of the new birth or regeneration begins, as with his treatment of justification, by reiterating the condition on fallen man. He begins with the Scripture teaching on man created in the image of God and then develops his anthropology from this cardinal doctrine. In language borrowed from Isaac Watts, he describes the *imago Dei* in man as having *natural*, *political* and *moral* dimensions. The natural image means that mankind is a picture of the divine immortality, having understanding, freedom of will and affections. The political image has reference to man being made the governor of this lower world and having dominion over all creatures. By the moral image is meant that God made man in righteousness and true holiness. As God is love and perfect purity, and as he is full of justice, mercy and truth, such was man when he came from the hand of God. But he was not made immutable and, when tempted, disobeyed God's commandment. In that day he died, died to God, lost the life of God and fellowship with God. And he lost the moral image in which he was made, that is, righteousness and holiness, though remnants of the political and natural image remained in his soul. In Adam, as Paul declares, 'all died,' all humanity is now in the image of fallen Adam. This, says Wesley, is the foundation of the biblical doctrine of the new birth; everyone born of woman needs to be born again of the Spirit of God.

Scripture alone gives us an account of what the new birth is, though not a minute, philosophical account of the *manner how* this is done. That's what Jesus meant when he said that although we know that the wind blows, we cannot explain its origins. We can give a scriptural account of the nature of the new birth and what it accomplishes in our souls, but not the *how* of that miracle. The analogy with natural birth, as Jesus used in conversation with Nicodemus, is to the effect that the child is born in a moment into a whole new environment and grows up into that new life. So it is with the man or woman born of the Spirit. This delineation of the doctrine of man's fall and universal sinfulness brings Wesley to the point of giving a formal definition of how he understands the new birth.

> It is that great change which God works in the souls when he brings it into life: when he raises it from the death of sin to the life of righteousness. It is the change wrought in the whole soul by the almighty Spirit of God, when it is "created anew in Christ Jesus."... In a word, it is that change whereby the "earthly, sensual, devilish" mind is turned into the mind which was "in Christ." This is the nature of the new birth.[106]

Wesley wants to insist that an inseparable part of the biblical doctrine of justification by faith is the parallel biblical doctrine of the new birth or regeneration. As often as he speaks of justification and regeneration together, and that is very often, he never fails to indicate that while justification is God doing something *for* us, regeneration is God doing something *in* us. By the former, we were once enemies to God now become his children; by the latter we who were sinners now become saints. Justification restores us to the favour of God, while regeneration restores us to the image of God. By the first the guilt of sin is cancelled; by the second the power of sin is broken.[107] As to the question why we need to be born again, Wesley's answer is explicit – it is necessary for holiness. Here Wesley is adding another important element to his *ordo salutis*. He has already argued for universal sinfulness, prevenient grace, justification by faith and regeneration by the Spirit. But, as he constantly insisted, by salvation he meant 'not barely (according to the vulgar notion) deliverance from hell, or going to heaven, but a present deliverance from sin, a restoration of the soul to its primitive health, its original purity; a recovery of the divine nature; the renewal of our souls after the image of God in righteousness and true holiness.'[108] Wesley's understanding of salvation not only embraces a doctrine of the sinner's new legal standing before God, but a corollary doctrine of his transformed character. He was fond of asserting that while other branches of Christendom often confused justification and

---

[106] John Wesley, *Works [BE],* Vol. 2, pp.193, 194.
[107] John Wesley, *Works [BE],* Vol. 1, p.432.
[108] John Wesley, *Works [BE],* Vol. 11, p.106.

sanctification, God had given the Methodists 'a full and clear knowledge of each.... They know indeed that at the same time a man is justified sanctification properly begins.'[109] In other words, in John Wesley's order of salvation, regeneration is sanctification begun; that is, it is the work of the Spirit transforming the justified Christian into a holy Christian. It is this correlation between John Wesley's doctrines of justification and sanctification that demands a thorough understanding of the former in order to appraise the latter. Wesley's doctrine of sanctification by faith is firmly grounded in his doctrine of justification by faith and a careful analysis of the former goes a long way in explaining the latter.

Whenever John Wesley declared his doctrine of regeneration or new birth, it always evoked criticism from those who held tenaciously to the Church of England's doctrine of baptism. It was the common understanding that in the sacrament of infant baptism, the child was made, in the words of the Catechism, 'a member of Christ, the child of God, and an inheritor of the kingdom of heaven.'[110] By any understanding of this description it surely meant spiritual regeneration. That John Wesley held this view of baptism can hardly be doubted, but the inferences he drew from it were very different from his Anglican contemporaries. He had no doubt at all that for the vast majority of those who had been baptised, the spiritual benefits of that good sacrament were long since lost. His riposte to those who made their baptism the reason for refusing the doctrine of the new birth was typically forthright.

> Say not in your heart, I *was once* baptised; therefore I *am now* a child of God. Alas, that consequence will by no means hold. How many are the baptised gluttons and drunkards, the baptised liars and common swearers, the baptised railers and evil speakers, the baptised whoremongers, thieves, extortioners! What think you? Are these now the children of God? Verily I say unto you, whosoever you are, unto whom any of the preceding characters belong, 'Ye are of your father

---

[109] John Wesley, *Works [BE],* Vol. 3, p.506.

[110] A Catechism, *The Book of Common Prayer*, p.289.

> the devil, and the works of your father ye do. Unto you I call in the name of him whom you crucify afresh, and in his words to your circumcised predecessors, 'Ye serpents, ye generation of vipers, how can you escape the damnation of hell?' How indeed, except ye be born again![111]

So far attention has been given to John Wesley's understanding of justification by faith and the inseparable concomitant of that doctrine, regeneration. Wesley interpreted regeneration in a way that made it the beginnings of sanctification and this insistence that the new birth is sanctification begun is an integral part of Wesley's doctrine of sanctification by faith. Before this doctrine is looked at in summary, one other element of Wesley's *ordo salutis* must not be neglected. This is his doctrine of assurance, or, as he usually referred to it, the witness of the Spirit.

From the beginning of John Wesley's post-Aldersgate preaching in May 1738, his emphasis on the privilege of the regenerate knowing this work in their souls is beyond question. His own testimony to what happened to him on that Wednesday evening, May 24, set the pattern. 'I felt I did trust in Christ, Christ alone for salvation, and an assurance was given me that he had taken away my sins, even mine, and saved me from the law of sin and death,'[112] Six months later he wrote to his elder brother Samuel, saying he believed that 'the witness of God's Spirit' should be expected and experienced by every justified believer.[113] In June 1744 he wrote to one of his preachers, arguing that without the witness of the Spirit no one is a true Christian.[114] The first issue of his published sermons in 1746 contained the first of two discourses entitled, *The Witness of the Spirit*, and the second was published in 1767. The first sermon attempted a formal definition of what this assurance is. 'The testimony of the Spirit is an inward impression on the soul, whereby the Spirit of God directly witnesses

[111] John Wesley, *Works [BE]*, Vol. 1, pp.428, 429.
[112] John Wesley, *Journals*, Vol. 18, pp.249-250.
[113] John Wesley, *Letters*, Vol. 1, pp.274, 275.
[114] John Wesley, *Letters*, Vol. 2, p.23.

to my spirit that I am a child of God; that Jesus Christ hath loved me, and given himself for me; that all my sins are blotted out, and I, even I, am reconciled to God.'[115] The second sermon on this theme repeated the definition and asserted that it should be the concern of Methodists to understand, explain and defend this doctrine because 'it is one grand part of the testimony which God has given them to bear to all mankind.'[116]

Wesley's correspondence in the 1740's with 'John Smith' dealt with the doctrines preached by the 'Methodists,' of which John Wesley was the acknowledged leader. 'John Smith' was a pseudonym for an unknown member of the Anglican clergy who was well read in divinity and Anglican history and practice. He had read John Wesley's *Journal* and wrote to Wesley, with dignity and restraint, on a number of issues. His second letter suggested that the Methodists preached 'perceptible inspiration,' that is, that Christians should enjoy a full assurance of forgiveness and eternal life here and now, and such teaching is not found in Scripture. Wesley replied to this charge and confessed that this assurance was a distinctive Methodist doctrine.

> Therefore the distinguishing doctrines on which I do insist in all my writings and in all my preaching will lie in a very narrow compass. You sum them all up in perceptible inspiration. For this I earnestly contend; and so do all who are called Methodist preachers. But be pleased to observe what we mean thereby. We mean that inspiration of God's Holy Spirit whereby he fills us with righteousness, peace, joy, with love to him and to all mankind. And we believe it cannot be, in the nature of things, that a man should be filled with this peace and joy and love by the inspiration of the Holy Spirit without perceiving it, as clearly as he does the light of the sun. This is the main doctrine of the Methodists. This is the substance of what we preach. And I will still believe, none is a true Christian till he experiences it... This is the point for which alone I contend. And this I take to be the very foundation of Christianity.[117]

---

[115] John Wesley, *Works [BE],* Vol. 1, p.274.
[116] John Wesley, *Works [BE],* Vol. 1, p.285.
[117] John Wesley, *Works [BE],* Vol. 26, pp.181, 182.

In 1762, William Warburton, Bishop of Gloucester, published an attack on John Wesley and the Methodists. He regarded them as fanatics and false prophets and lampooned them as deceivers of the people. Wesley spent five days in writing his reply to Warburton's attacks, and emphasised especially that it is the work of the Spirit to regenerate sinners. It is also the work of the Spirit to renew believers in grace, to conquer sin and bring about their sanctification. In support of these operations of the Spirit Wesley quoted at length from Bishop Pearson's, *Exposition of the Creed.* Pearson had said all that Wesley wanted to say, including a very clear statement on the witness of the Spirit.' It is also the office of the Holy Ghost to assure us of the adoption of sons... As, therefore, we are born again by the Spirit, and receive from Him our regeneration, so we are also by the same Spirit assured of our adoption.'[118] Wesley then posed a question to Bishop Warburton. 'It now rests with your Lordship to take your choice, either to condemn or to acquit both; either your Lordship must condemn Bishop Pearson for an enthusiast, or you must acquit me; for I have his express authority on my side concerning every text which I affirm to belong to all Christians.'[119] Wesley had found an ally in one of his Church's greatest theologians in support of his doctrine of the witness of the Spirit.

Wesley's answers to both 'John Smith' and Bishop Warburton make it very clear that he believed every justified person has the assurance of their acceptance by God. He made this point incontrovertible when he added that 'none is a true Christian' until he has this assurance. In his, *Farther Appeal*, he spoke again of assurance as necessary for justification. 'The moment a penitent sinner believes this [Christ dying for him], God pardons and absolves him. And as soon as his pardon or justification is witnessed to him by the Holy Ghost, he is saved.'[120] The 1746 sermon, *The Witness of the Spirit*, goes into great detail in explaining what this witness is. Although it does not say so explicitly,

---

[118] John Wesley, *Letters*, Vol. 4, pp.377, 378.

[119] John Wesley, *Letters*, Vol. 4, p.378.

[120] John Wesley, *A Father Appeal to Men of Reason and Religion*, Works, Vol. 8, p.107.

the impression is that the witness of the Spirit is the gift of God given at the time of justification.

A few years later John Wesley's emphasis on the necessity of assurance for salvation was shifting significantly. In a long letter to his brother Charles, while he admits that an assurance of sins forgiven is 'the common privilege of real Christians,' yet it is not 'necessarily connected' to justifying faith. To say it is would mean that all who do not have it are still under condemnation, and that is contrary to both Scripture and Christian experience. The Methodists have been blessed by God in preaching the great truths of the gospel, although, admits Wesley, 'we tacked to them, in the simplicity of our hearts, a proposition which was not true.'[121] This was a clear acknowledgement that the earlier insistence that justifying faith must be accompanied by the witness of the Spirit to the Christian's heart was now no longer advocated. John made this admission in 1747, yet, surprisingly, it is not reflected in his second sermon, *The Witness of the Spirit*, published in 1767. In this sermon Wesley quotes his earlier definition on the witness of the Spirit, 'an inward impression on the soul...' and adds that after twenty years he sees no cause to retract anything he had written earlier. Wesley asserts that so clear and convincing is the New Testament doctrine of the witness of the Spirit that any denial of it is tantamount to denying justification by faith.[122] While the sermon stops short of making the testimony of the Spirit a necessary concomitant of justification, yet it is spoken of as the common experience of all who are truly justified.

A year after he published this sermon, John Wesley found himself embroiled in another controversy with another Anglican antagonist. Five years earlier, Thomas Rutherforth, Regius Professor Divinity at Cambridge and Archdeacon of Essex, had attacked the Methodists by name in his, *Four Charges*. He dismissed them for parading themselves as Anglicans when they were really Dissenters, for

[121] John Wesley, *Letters*, Vol. 2, pp.108, 109.
[122] John Wesley, *Works [BE],* Vol. 1, p.292.

allowing anyone to preach and for propagating 'enthusiasm.' Wesley did not see Rutherforth's book until 1768 and he answered it right away. He gave particular attention to the doctrine of the witness of the Spirit, for he knew that Rutherforth's attacks represented what many of the clergy thought about Methodist doctrine. What he wrote was an understanding of various levels of assurance, rather than an assertion that all Christians experience the same degree of the 'inner witness.' Most justified Christians enjoy such an assurance of being accepted in Christ that it excludes all doubt and fear. There are still other Christians who have such an assurance but it is frequently interrupted by doubt or fear. Also there are exceptions to this general rule. Possibly some true believers are still in mourning and unsure of being in the favour of God, but this is due either to bodily infirmity or 'ignorance of the gospel promises.' 'Therefore I have not for many years thought a consciousness of acceptance to be essential to justifying faith.'[123]

This considered reply to Rutherforth could be considered John Wesley's mature thinking on the doctrine of the witness of the Spirit. There are variations of experience among the people of God and, in particular, a lack of assurance or spiritual certainty my not necessarily indicate defective Christian experience. While it is clear that Wesley's thinking on this subject developed over the years, yet there were three constants he maintained on this distinctive Methodist doctrine. First, the witness of the Spirit to sins forgiven and acceptance with God is the common privilege of all Christians and should be prayerfully expected. Second, the Spirit not only witnesses to the work of justification but likewise to the on-going work of regeneration and sanctification throughout the Christian's life. Third, the testimony of the Spirit will always be supported by the fruit of the Spirit. If claim is laid to a personal witness of the Spirit concerning justification and sins forgiven, then the authenticity of that claim will always be confirmed by the marks of the Spirit in holy living.

[123] John Wesley, *Letters*, Vol. 5, pp.358, 359.

Earlier in this chapter attention was drawn to the understanding of salvation delineated by John Wesley early in the Revival. 'By salvation I mean a present deliverance from sin, a restoration of the soul to its primitive health, its original purity; a recovery of the divine nature; the renewal of our souls after the image of God in righteousness and true holiness.'[124] In reality, John Wesley had embarked on a lifelong pursuit of holiness understood as the image of God stamped on the soul and showing itself in love to God and man. The doctrine of Christian holiness that emerged from his writings was not just one element in his theological system; it was a foundation of all his thinking about God, and grace and salvation. The doctrine of sanctification that became linked with his name was no mere appendage to his creed, for there is the clearest evidence that he was seeking holiness of heart and life before he fully understood, and certainly before he experienced, justification by faith. He traced the beginnings of the Methodist movement to his own and his brother Charles' search for the secret of holy living. To the question posed at the first Conference in 1744, 'What was the rise of Methodism, so called?' the answer was:

> In 1729, two young men, reading the Bible, saw they could not be saved without holiness, followed after it, and incited others so to do. In 1737 they saw holiness comes by faith. They saw likewise, that men are justified before they are sanctified; but still holiness was their point. God then thrust them out, utterly against their will, to raise a holy people.[125]

At a later Conference the question was asked, 'What may we reasonably believe to be God's design in raising up the Preachers called Methodists?' The answer was: 'Not to form any new sect; but to reform the nation, particularly the Church; and to spread scriptural holiness over the land.' The dates given in the first answer are very significant. Wesley saw 1729 as the year that witnessed the birth of the movement in Oxford that would emerge as 'Methodism.' In that year he had returned from assisting his father in Epworth and had joined the small group already organised by Charles Wesley. As they met

---

[124] John Wesley, *Works [BE],* Vol. 11, p.106.
[125] John Wesley, *Works*, Vol. 8, p.300.

regularly for prayer and other devotional exercises, they became convinced that to be saved meant being holy. This was a discovery that would influence John Wesley's thinking for the rest of his life. Being 'saved' did not merely mean forgiveness, or even the certainty of eternal life – it meant being holy. Whatever biblical and theological refinements this understanding would undergo in the next six decades, the core truth would remain central to John Wesley's creed – God has made provision for his people to live holy lives.

The second date noted in Wesley's account is equally significant. 'In 1737 they saw holiness comes by faith. They saw likewise that men are justified before they are sanctified.'[126] In 1737 both John and Charles Wesley were in Georgia and in close fellowship with the Moravians and their cardinal Lutheran doctrine of salvation by faith. The Moravian influence would climax for both brothers in May 1738, following which both of them would make salvation by faith the cornerstone of their preaching. John Wesley confessed in later years that, prior to his meeting with the Moravians, he thought of the Christian life in terms of faith in the propositional truths of Scripture, accompanied by scrupulous self-examination and dedicated holy living. The year 1737 is highlighted as the year of the momentous discovery – that justification precedes sanctification in Christian experience. As he grappled with a new understanding of salvation by faith early in 1738, he strongly reprimanded William Law for not having instructed him properly in this cardinal doctrine. All the evidence from John Wesley's writings concerning 'Oxford Methodism' point to one conclusion – Wesley and his earnest fellow 'Methodists' were sincerely and devoutly seeking sanctification of heart and life without the foundation of justification by faith. Following the momentous spiritual events of Pentecost 1738, John Wesley took great care, both in preaching and writing, to demonstrate his conviction that sanctification, understood as holiness of heart and life, is realisable only for those already enjoying justification by faith and the regenerating power of the Holy Spirit. The years 1737 and

[126] John Wesley, *Works*, Vol. 8, p.300.

1738 mark the time when John Wesley's thinking on Christian holiness shifted most decidedly. The move was away from his earlier pre-occupation with the kind of high Anglican theology of sanctification found in the writings of Jeremy Taylor and other advocates of the 'holy living' school, to a more biblical perspective of justification as the only foundation for all true Christian experience.

When John Wesley came to write his definitive treatise on Christian holiness in 1766, *A Plain Account of Christian Perfection*, his opening paragraphs detailed the help he had received from the writings of Jeremy Taylor, Thomas a'Kempis and William Law. He had read these works between 1725 and 1729 and was deeply moved by their insistence on 'inward holiness.' Years later when he was defending his doctrine of Christian perfection, he again expressed his debt to Taylor, a'Kempis and Law. How can that be reconciled with his statement that he did not 'discover' the truth that justification precedes sanctification until 1737? The answer to that question will help to explain Wesley's own spiritual journey in the late 1730's and account for the main elements in his subsequent doctrine of Christian perfection.

In the writings of Taylor, a'Kempis and Law, John Wesley found the ideal of the holy life. These spiritual writers inspired him, in the works of his later account, 'to be all devoted to God in body, soul and spirit.'[127] Then he began to study the Bible, as distinct from merely reading it, and there he found those New Testament characterisations of holiness that he would employ throughout his life. They included the Pauline descriptions, 'the mind which was in Christ,' and 'walking as Christ also walked.' When he preached his 1733 university sermon, *The Circumcision of the Heart*,[128] it reflected these teachings. Inspired by the words of the Collect for that day, (the Feast of the Circumcision of Christ) 'Grant us the true circumcision of the spirit...' he preached this spiritual circumcision as the perfect love of God and neighbour. Thirty two years later he claimed that his 1733 sermon contained 'all

---

[127] John Wesley, *Letters*, Vol. 4, p.299.
[128] John Wesley, *Works [BE],* Vol. 1, pp.398-414.

that I now teach concerning salvation from all sin and loving God with an undivided heart.'[129] This means that his Oxford sermon expressed his understanding of the ideal of the holy life; that is, the love of God and man. From that ideal he never departed and everything he wrote subsequently on holiness had love perfected as its kernel truth.

What, then, did he discover, according to his own account, in 1737? He discovered the dynamic of holy living; it is the fruit of justification by faith and the regenerating energy of the Holy Spirit. The ideal of the holy life was firmly fixed in John Wesley's thinking from 1725 onwards; he discovered the secret and dynamic of holy living in the late 1730's. If any proof of this was needed, it is supplied by the words he added to his 1733 sermon when he published it in 1748. He did not remove or alter any of the previous wording but added a very significant paragraph. Speaking of the faith that overcomes the world, Wesley had described it as an 'unshaken assent' to every truth found in Scripture, and particularly the truth that Christ came to save sinners and to make propitiation for universal sin. Now came the additional paragraph.

> Likewise the revelation of Christ in our hearts; a divine evidence or conviction of his love, his free, unmerited love to me a sinner; a sure confidence whereby every true believer is enabled to bear witness, 'I know that my Redeemer liveth;' that I 'have an advocate with the Father,' that 'Jesus Christ the righteous is *my* Lord,' and, 'the propitiation for my sins.' I know he 'hath loved *me*, and given himself for me.' He 'hath reconciled *me*, even me to God;' and I 'have redemption through his blood, even the forgiveness of sins.'[130]

Commenting on this added paragraph, Albert Outler says: 'In 1732 Wesley was still preoccupied with holy living. Here, in 1748, he has added his discovery of justifying faith as unmerited mercy and as the assurance of forgiveness through the merits of Christ's propitiatory

---

[129] John Wesley, *Letters*, Vol. 4, p.299.
[130] John Wesley, *Works [BE],* Vol. 1, p.405.

death.[131] Anglican theologians of the 'holy living' tradition whom Wesley admired so much had all contributed to his understanding of the ideal life of holiness, but they had not pointed him to the all-important foundation of justification by faith. Jeremy Taylor's, *Holy Living* and *Dying*, a'Kempis's, *Imitatione*, and Law's *Serious Call* and *Christian Perfection* – and John Wesley's 1733 Oxford sermon – all delineate the holy life in a most convincing and stimulating way but they do not show the *way* of salvation.

Having brought his ideal of holiness as the love of God and man to his discovery of the way of justification in the late 1730's, it was inevitable that Wesley's resultant doctrine of salvation would make holiness of heart and life the consequence of a right relationship with God. Put another way, it was impossible for John Wesley, post 1738, to think of any concept of salvation that did not naturally lead to a holy life. Although he never forsook the Reformation doctrine of salvation *sola fidei*, he saw that its over-emphasis could lead to *fideism*. When this happened, justification, as merely a forensic concept, lost the biblical doctrine of regeneration and failed to proclaim sanctification as the fruit of justification. For that reason John Wesley began to give pointed emphasis to the place of good work in the Christian life; good works, not as the basis of justifying faith but as its direct consequence. Otherwise, he replied to his critics, the door is opened wide to Antinomianism.

It was for these reasons that after 1738, and especially from the 1760's onwards, John Wesley always spoke of salvation in terms of justification and sanctification. To reverse the order or neglect sanctification as the consequence of justification, was, he believed, a misinterpretation of Scripture. That resulted, inevitably, either in Pharisaism or Antinomianism. What God had joined together must not be put asunder. Biblical salvation meant not only a new relationship with God (justification) but it also meant sanctification, the believer being transformed into the likeness of Christ. One of Wesley's fullest

---

[131] Albert Outler, *Works [BE],* Vol.1, p.405, footnote.

and most comprehensive soteriological sermons was published in 1765, *The Scripture Way of Salvation*. It was a definitive declaration of how John Wesley understood salvation.

> What is salvation? [It] consists of two general parts, justification and sanctification. Justification is the forgiveness of all our sins... and the immediate effects are, the peace of God... and a 'rejoicing in hope of the glory of God.' ...And at the same time that we are justified, yea, in that very moment, sanctification begins. In that instant we are 'born again,' 'born from above,' 'born of the Spirit.' There is a *real* as well as a relative *change*. We are inwardly renewed by the power of God... From the time of our being 'born again' the gradual work of sanctification takes place... It is thus we wait for entire sanctification, for a full salvation from all our sins... It is love excluding sin.[132]

[132] John Wesley, *Works [BE]*, Vol. 2, pp.156-160.

LECTURE 3
JOHN WESLEY AND CHRISTIAN HOLINESS

Near the end of his life, John Wesley wrote to one of his preachers and raised the question of Christian holiness, 'I am glad Brother Dieuiside has more light with regard to full sanctification. This doctrine is the grand depositum which God has lodged with the people called Methodists, and for the sake of propagating this chiefly He appeared to have raised us up.'[133] By 'full sanctification' Wesley meant the doctrine also known as scriptural holiness, entire sanctification, Christian holiness, love perfected, the great salvation, and other descriptions. Here, late in life, he had not changed his opinion about its importance, for he designated it as the depositum or that particular Scripture emphasis he believed the Methodists had received from the Lord. He also believed it was their privilege and responsibility to disseminate this truth across the land. Many years earlier, at one of the annual Conferences with his preachers, the question had been asked; 'What may we reasonably believe to be God's design in raising up the Preachers called Methodists?' The formal answer was: 'To reform the nation, particularly the Church, and to spread scriptural holiness over the land.'[134] This chapter will examine what John Wesley meant by 'scriptural holiness.'

As with most of Wesley's doctrinal convictions, the beginnings of his interest in Christian holiness are to be found in his years at Oxford University. As he prepared himself for ordination in 1725, he sought to give his whole life to God, prompted by reading Jeremy Taylor's *Holy Living*. 'I began to alter the whole form of my conversation, and to set in earnest upon a new life... I began to aim at, and pray for, inward holiness.'[135] This search for what he later called 'the religion of the heart,' marked the beginning of a spiritual pilgrimage for John Wesley that engaged him for the rest of his life. When, some years later, he

---

[133] John Wesley, *Letters*, Vol. 8, p.238.
[134] John Wesley, *Works*, Vol. 8, p.300.
[135] John Wesley, *Works*, Vol. 18, p.244.

came to an understanding of what he believed was the biblical relationship between justification and sanctification, he began to preach sanctification by faith as the goal of all Christians in this life. The year 1729 marked the beginning of the movement at Oxford, led by John Wesley, that was dubbed 'Methodism.' John Wesley acknowledged that it was the passion for personal holiness that marked the spiritual devotion of this group from the very beginning. This was 'the rise of Methodism, so called.'

> In 1729, two young men, reading the Bible, saw they could not be saved without holiness, followed after it, and incited others so to do. In 1737 they saw holiness comes by faith. They saw likewise, that men are justified before they are sanctified; but still holiness was their point. God then thrust them out, utterly against their will, to raise a holy people.[136]

This summary statement drew attention to the great change that took place in John Wesley's theological thinking in the late 1730's. Until the significance of this admission is grasped, Wesley's theology of holiness cannot be understood. The 'two young men' were, of course, his brother Charles and himself. John had returned to Oxford from assisting his father at Epworth and joined the small group organised by Charles. From the beginning salvation and holiness were concomitant truths. When Wesley said they knew they could not be saved without holiness, he meant that they understood salvation not merely in terms of forgiveness but also in terms of holy living. This understanding would become a constant in John Wesley's theology. To be saved in the biblical sense is to be justified, that is, forgiven, but it also means to be sanctified, to be given grace to live a holy life here and now. In John Wesley's writings the word 'holiness,' in relation to men and women, always means the state of being made like Christ. It means to be cleansed from inner sins such as pride, self-will and love of the world, and to become like Christ in all the conduct of life. On many occasions John Wesley wrote that this understanding of holiness was impressed upon him, not only as he studied the Bible, but as he read, in particular, the writings of Jeremy Taylor, Thomas a'Kempis and

---

[136] John Wesley, *Works*, Vol. 8, p.300.

William Law. These writers stressed 'the religion of the heart.' That is, the need and possibility of being saved from the dominion of sin and living a holy life.

Taking these writers in particular as their spiritual guides, the Oxford 'Methodists' embarked on a sincere attempt to put their teaching into practice. They sought to avoid all known sin, they attended Holy Communion with strict regularity, they engaged in good works of many kinds and they met in small groups for prayer, the study of the Bible and mutual encouragement. They were setting out with the deliberate intention of living holy lives. John Wesley's 1733 Oxford sermon, 'The Circumcision of the Heart' is a summary of the kind of holiness they were ardently pursuing. He described it as 'that habitual disposition of soul which, in the sacred writings, is termed holiness;' and which directly implies the being cleansed from sin, 'from all filthiness both of flesh and spirit,' and, by consequence, the being endued with those virtues which were also in Christ Jesus; the being so 'renewed in the spirit of our mind' as to be 'perfect as our Father in heaven is perfect.'[137] All the main elements of Wesley's later doctrine of Christian holiness are found in this description. Holiness is being cleansed from inner sin, it is having the virtues of Christ and it can be called perfection.

Justification and Sanctification

It was with this understanding of holiness that John Wesley continued to lead the Oxford Methodists until he left for Georgia in October 1735. It was there that he came into close contact with German evangelicals, the Moravians. As his admiration of their Christian testimony increased, he came more and more under the influence of their essentially Lutheran doctrine of justification by faith. He began to be convinced that while Oxford Methodism lacked nothing in its devotion and sincerity, it had missed something of great importance. It was seeking sanctification without the necessary foundation of

[137] John Wesley, *Works [BE]*, Vol. 1, pp.402, 403.

justification. Now, under Moravian influence, Wesley is beginning to understand that theologically he had inverted the Scripture order. In the devout practice of sanctification he hoped to be justified. This was a Copernican shift in John Wesley's theology. He was now convinced he knew why the strict and sincere regime of the Oxford Methodists had not given him the inner peace, the victory over all sin and the sense of acceptance with God he had so long sought. Without the experience of personal justification, sanctification must always remain elusive. John Wesley was learning what he would later stress so strongly, that our sins must be forgiven by the grace of justification before the work of inner sanctification can take place.

Under the strain of this all-important discovery, John Wesley remained in Georgia until December 1737 and then prepared to return to England. On the homeward journey he wrote a kind of spiritual memorandum that highlighted his agony of spirit and his search for spiritual certainty. 'The faith I want is a "sure trust and confidence in God, that, through the merits of Christ, my sins are forgiven, and I reconciled to the favour of God"... I want that faith which none can have without knowing that he hath it... for whosoever hath it, is "freed from sin... is freed from fear... is freed from doubt."'[138] This search for justification and assurance was intensified when Wesley met the Moravian Peter Bohler in London in February 1738, and it climaxed in the 'heart-warming' of Aldersgate Street on May 24 that year. John Wesley's testimony to the events of that evening is revealing. 'An assurance was given me that he had taken away my sins, even mine, and saved me from the law of sin and death.'[139] That evening in Aldersgate Street Wesley found what he had been seeking so long – the sense of inner assurance. He now knew in experience what he had learned the previous year from the Moravians – justification by faith is the foundation of all Christian experience.

---

[138] John Wesley, *Works [BE],* Vol. 18, pp.215, 216.
[139] John Wesley, *Works [BE],* Vol. 18, p.250.

Some writers dealing with Wesley's theology and experience have hinted that May 24 was relatively unimportant in his spiritual pilgrimage. Indeed Maximin Piette even suggested that if John Wesley had not recorded it in his *Journal* he would probably have forgotten all about it. This is very far from the truth. The conviction that justification must precede sanctification came to John Wesley in 1737, it was reinforced by personal experience in May 1738 and it continued to be the foundation of his preaching for the next fifty years. The correlation that Wesley saw between justification and sanctification is all-important for his doctrine of sanctification. In relation to the sinner's condition before God, Wesley has a very clear *order* of salvation. In justification the *guilt* of sin is cancelled and the sinner is reconciled to God. He is now a Christian and no longer under condemnation. But justification does not stand alone. It is accompanied by regeneration in which the *power* of sin is broken. And justification is sanctification begun and in sanctification the *in-being* of sin (as Wesley called it) is rendered inoperative. It is counter-acted by a superior power, the love of God, and where love holds sway, sin no longer prevails.

Before John Wesley's claims about the extent of sanctification in this life are looked at more closely, it is necessary to see how consistently he preached and wrote of sanctification as the fruit of justification. Some of his clear statements on this correlation must be noted. When he published his sermon, *The New Birth,* in 1760, he explained it as regeneration, by which the sinner is raised from spiritual death into life and renewed in righteousness. But the new birth is not sanctification. 'When we are born again, then our sanctification, our inward and outward holiness begins.'[140] The new birth is a miracle of grace that occurs in a moment; sanctification is a process. Wesley says there is an 'exact analogy' here between natural and spiritual happenings. In a moment a baby is born and this is followed by many years of growing to maturity. Likewise the sinner is 'born again' in a moment and then by slow degrees grows up to the full stature of Christian maturity.[141]

---

[140] John Wesley, *Works [BE],* Vol. 2, p.198.
[141] John Wesley, *Works [BE],* Vol. 2, p.198.

This point was made with even more emphasis in Wesley's 1765 sermon, *The Scripture Way of Salvation.* He defined salvation, in its broadest sense, 'as all the work of God in the human soul from the dawning of prevenient grace to final glory. But present salvation consists of two general parts, justification and sanctification.'[142] Justification is pardon for sins committed while sanctification is the filling of the Christian's heart with love in order to expel all sin. 'From the time of our being 'born again,' the gradual work of sanctification takes place. We are enabled by the Spirit to "mortify the deeds of he body," of our evil nature... It is thus that we wait for entire sanctification, for a full salvation from all our sins, from pride, self-will, anger, unbelief.'[143] Clearly for John Wesley justification is the work of a moment; sanctification is the work of a lifetime. Justification means pardon for sins; sanctification means the death of sin. Justification brings about for the sinner a new judicial standing before God because he is pardoned and reconciled. Sanctification brings about a new state of actual holiness because he is being cleansed from inner pollution and restored to the image of God.

This correlation between justification and sanctification was spelt out very plainly in Wesley's 1785 sermon, *On Working Out Your Own Salvation.* Again the emphasis is on the soteriological relationship between justification and sanctification, with the latter as the inevitable outworking of the former. 'The proper Christian salvation [consists] of those two grand branches, justification and sanctification. By justification we are saved from the guilt of sin, and restored to the favour of God. By sanctification we are saved from the power and root of sin and restored to the image of God.'[144] Two years later Wesley reasoned that while there was much confusion among Christians concerning the relationship between justification and sanctification, the 'Methodists' know better.

---

142 John Wesley, *Works [BE],* Vol. 2, p.158.
143 John Wesley, *Works [BE],* Vol. 2, p.160.
144 John Wesley, *Works [BE],* Vol. 3, p.204.

> It has pleased God to give the Methodists a full and clear knowledge of each, and the wide difference between them. They know, indeed, that at the same time a man is justified sanctification properly begins. For when he is justified he is 'born again,' 'born from above,' 'born of the Spirit,' which, although it is not the whole process of sanctification, it is doubtless the gate of it... The new birth, therefore, is the first point of sanctification, which may increase more and more unto the perfect day... They do not think or speak of justification so as to supersede sanctification, so neither do they think or speak of sanctification so as to supersede justification... They maintain with equal zeal and diligence the doctrine of free, full, present justification on the one hand, and of entire sanctification both of heart and life on the other.[145]

Christian Holiness Defined

As early as 1733 John Wesley defined holiness as the process by which the human heart is cleansed from sin and so endued with the virtues of Christ that the Christian is perfect.[146] From 1738 onwards, while this understanding of perfection or Christian holiness was buttressed by Wesley's new emphasis on justification by faith, holiness continued to be understood as cleaning from sin and renewal in the image of God. In what he described as his 'first tract' on perfection, Wesley spoke of 'perfect' Christians as those believers who, having found redemption through the blood of Christ, now love God with all their heart. They love their neighbours as themselves, their hearts are fixed on God and their souls are 'holiness unto the Lord.' Then Wesley made the emphasis that would become a constant theme in his writings – the love of God in the heart is demonstrated by holy obedience. These Christians keep all the commandments of God, they are 'inwardly and outwardly conformed to the will of God,' and in all things they walk as Christ 'also walked.'[147]

---

[145] John Wesley, *Works [BE],* Vol. 3, pp.506-507.
[146] John Wesley, *Works [BE],* Vol. 1, pp.402, 403.
[147] John Wesley, *Works [BE],* Vol. 9, 'The Character of a Methodist,' pp.35-41.

As early as this 1739 tract, *The Character of a Methodist*, John Wesley was advocating holiness as a purity of heart that issued in holy living. He admitted that he had purposely not used the word 'perfection' in the tract because of the prejudice it occasioned, but two years later he wrote his first full sermon on Christian holiness and published it under the title, *Christian Perfection*. The selected texts were Phil. 3:12 and 15, 'Not as though I had already attained or were already perfect... Let us therefore, as many as are perfect.' Although Wesley admits that the term 'perfect' causes reproach and confusion, yet no preacher has the right to ignore a scriptural word, and the sermon proposes to show in what ways Christians are not perfect and in what ways they can be perfect. They are not perfect in knowledge and the holiest of men and women will be subject to error and ignorance in many things while they are on earth. Neither are Christians delivered from infirmities in this life and Wesley tries to define infirmity in a way that does not excuse sin. An infirmity is any of those 'outward or inward imperfections which are not of a moral nature.'[148] While Wesley thinks of sin in terms of moral transgression, viz. breaking God's commandments, he thinks of infirmities in terms of all those deficiencies that belong to mental, emotional and physical humanness. This is a very important distinction for John Wesley's doctrine of Christian holiness. He never balked at claiming that Christians can be saved from all sin in this life but infirmities are not sins. In addition to these disclaimers, Wesley added that Christians are never free from temptation in this life. As Christ was tempted, even so all those who are fully sanctified are still vulnerable to temptation.

Having attempted to prove from Scripture that Christian holiness exists side by side with ignorance, error, infirmity and temptation, Wesley then offers a definition. The word 'perfection' is simply 'another term for holiness. They are two names for the same thing. Thus everyone that is perfect is holy, and everyone that is holy is, in the Scripture sense, perfect.'[149] When Wesley proceeds to speak of the ways in

---

[148] John Wesley, *Works [BE]*, Vol. 2, p.103.
[149] John Wesley, *Works [BE]*, Vol. 2, p.104.

which Christians are perfect in this life, he resorts to the Johannine description of believers as little children, young men and fathers. He sees these designations as referring to those newly born again, those who are more advanced in Christian experience, and the 'fathers' as those who are mature in the faith. The description 'perfect' is applicable only to these. They are perfect, Wesley affirms, in that they 'do not commit sin' where sin is understood as deliberate transgression. Wesley's defence for this assertion is the words of 1 John 3-9. 'Whosoever is born of God doth not commit sin, for his seed remaineth in him and he cannot sin.' And Wesley will not tolerate any amelioration of this stark declaration. While most biblical exegetes, in all ages of the Church, have interpreted this verse to mean that the Christian does not sin habitually, Wesley declares that there is no such explanation provided in the Scripture text. Even when it is pointed out that the men and women of faith found in the Bible sometimes fell into sin, Wesley's love of logic-chopping provides a ready answer. Because this or that man of God, in either the Old or New Testament, sinned, that does not mean that every Christian must sin. Salvation for Wesley is always salvation *from* sin, whether as inner corruption or as outward behaviour.

Wesley then declares his conclusion. 'In conformity therefore both to the doctrine of St. John, and to the whole tenor of the New Testament, we fix this conclusion: "A Christian is so far perfect as not to commit sin."'[150] By 'sin' Wesley meant any transgression of God's law, any breaking of the commandments. But he also meant more than that, for he went on to say that Christians are saved, not only from sinful actions, but also from all sinful thoughts. He distinguished between a sinful thought and a thought of sin. The former occurs when the mind is occupied with a sinful desire, concentrates the attention on it and contemplates the sinful action what will follow when the will concurs. A thought of sin, on the other hand, is when the mind conceives a sinful action but there is no desire to put it into action. Wesley illustrates by saying a Christian might think about a murder that has been committed

[150] John Wesley, *Works [BE]*, Vol. 2, p.116.

but he has not the least desire in his own heart to commit this sin. The Christian's heart is purified from all evil thoughts and Wesley is sure that this is what Scriptures teaches. He quotes 1 John 3:3 as reinforcing this truth. 'Everyone that hath this hope in him purifieth himself, even as he is pure.' As Christ is pure in heart, Wesley argues, so are all those who are true believers. Earlier in the letter John had spoken of the blood of Christ cleansing 'from all sin' (1:7). Wesley reads this to mean not merely a judicial deliverance from the guilt of sin but an actual deliverance from sin in the heart. He knows that two verses from the first chapter of John's letter will be quoted against this interpretation. 'If we say we have no sin we deceive ourselves... If we say we have not sinned we make him a liar...' His answer is that these verses are a warning against any claim that men and women have no sin to be cleansed from. All men have sinned and all need forgiveness, but these disavowals are not directed against those believers who have experienced the cleansing from 'all sin' that is promised in verse 7.

What is surprisingly absent from this 1741 sermon is any emphasis on Christian holiness as the perfection of love. Wesley wrote later that as a result of a meeting he had with Bishop Edmund Gibson late in 1740, he wrote this sermon. When he had explained to the bishop what he meant by perfection, Gibson told him to 'publish it to all the world.' There was, however, another event at this time that was occupying much of John Wesley's attention. There was a growing rift between the Moravians and himself and in part it was occasioned by the Moravians' unhappiness by Wesley's insistence on a doctrine of Christian perfection. In September 1741 Wesley had a meeting with the Moravian leader, Count Zinzendorf, in London, in which Zinzendorf made it very plain that he thought Wesley's teaching on holiness heretical. The Moravian teaching, in line with Luther's dictum that the Christian, though justified, is always a sinner, strongly repudiated Wesley's suggestion that the Christian could be delivered from all inner sin in this life. The Christian must struggle all his life against 'the old man' of man and any notion of a complete deliverance this side of death is a dangerous illusion. John Wesley's sermon in 1741 bears all the marks of being his attempt to define Christian perfection against the strictures of the Moravians.

In 1766 Wesley published, *A Plain Account of Christian Perfection*. Answering charges of contradictions and inconsistencies in his teaching, he put together selections from his publications over a period of more than thirty years. There was very little original material in the, *Plain Account,* and because he revised it in three subsequent editions, it can be read as his definitive apologia for Christian holiness. The various emphases that Wesley made in the, *Plain Account,* illustrate what could be called the summary points of this doctrine.
First, Wesley describes it as 'inward and outward holiness,' by which he means that the fully sanctified Christian is not only saved from all open sins of the flesh, but is also delivered from all inner sin, that is, from inner corruption. This means that because the heart is pure, the conduct is consequently pure. Perfection is not in terms of the perfection enjoyed by angels, or unfallen Adam or the perfection that belongs to final glorification. It is the image of God stamped on the heart which means that the indwelling Spirit renews the Christian in righteousness. Between the years 1752 and 1759 Wesley had further explained Christian holiness in terms of it being the love of God and man and attainable in this life.

> Christian perfection is that love of God and our neighbour, which implies deliverance from all sin. It is received merely by faith. It is given instantaneously, in one moment. We are to expect it, not at death, but every moment... [It is] the loving God with all our heart, mind, soul and strength. This implies that no wrong temper, none contrary to love, remains in the soul; that all the thoughts, words, and actions are governed by pure love.[151]

This claim to a perfection of love does not exclude the Christian's need for Christ's mediatorial work. He is united to Christ as the branch is united to the tree and all his holiness is derivative. Sin, defined as 'a voluntary transgression of a known law,' needs to be repented of and is forgiven by the virtue of Christ's atonement. But the sanctified

---

[151] John Wesley, *Works*, XI, pp.393, 394.

Christian is never fully delivered in this life from what Wesley calls 'involuntary transgressions.' These are the results of ignorance and mortality but because they do not have the consent of the will, Wesley does not label them as 'sins.' Yet, because they are transgressions of the perfect law, they require an atonement. This explanation is at the heart of John Wesley's dilemma on Christian perfection. He is certain that only those actions which have the consent of the will can be termed 'sins.' At the same time he knows that all fully sanctified Christians are guilty of 'involuntary transgressions,' and while these do not have the consent of the will and are not, therefore properly called 'sins,' yet they need atonement. It is for this reason, he argues, that he never uses the phrase 'sinless perfection' for that would suggest a state of grace in which the Christian is entirely delivered even from these involuntary transgressions.[152]

Having delineated Christian perfection as inward and outward holiness, the, *Plain Account,* then advanced the argument that it was neither more nor less than the love of God and neighbour. For John Wesley, this is 'the simple scriptural account... Pure love reigning alone in the heart and life – this is the whole of scriptural perfection.'[153] While it was noted that this emphasis is surprisingly missing from the 1741 sermon, 'Christian perfection,' it is important to see that from the early 1760's onward, it is Wesley's most constant and emphatic description of scriptural holiness. It occurs with constancy in his writings on the subject in the three decades from 1760 to 1790. The impression is that, had it not been for misunderstanding from within his own Societies, and strong, often virulent, opposition from the Calvinistic Methodists, Wesley would have been content to define scriptural perfection simply as the love of God and neighbour. Misunderstanding and persistent criticism forced him to further doctrinal definitions but his instinct was always to understand holiness in terms of Christ's Great Commandment. 'Thou shalt love the Lord

---

[152] John Wesley, *Works*, XI, p.396.
[153] John Wesley, *Works*, XI, p.401.

thy God with all thy heart... soul... mind... and... thy neighbour as thyself' (Matt. 22:37-39).

Scriptural perfection in terms of perfected love was important to Wesley both in terms of how he understood the law/gospel relationship and his definition of sin. Adam, in his unfallen state, was under obligation to render perfect obedience to God, and, like the angels this was within his capacity. But Adam fell into rebellion and sin, a sin that captivated the whole human race. Later, at Sinai, God instituted another covenant, represented by the moral law, the Ten Commandments. 'It is he whom in his essence no man hath seen or can see, made visible to men and angels. It is the face of God unveiled; God manifested to his creatures as they are able to bear it; manifested to give and not to destroy life; that that may see God and live. It is the heart of God disclosed to men.'[154] This law cannot save us by its own spiritual incentive; instead it is 'our schoolmaster unto Christ. It was destined to train us up for Christ. And this it did, both by its commands, which showed the need we had of his atonement, and its ceremonies which all pointed us to him.'[155] As the instrument of salvation, Christ has established a new law, the law of faith. Wesley then summarised his understanding of how justifying and sanctifying faith produces holy, obedient love in the Christian's heart.

> Not every one that doeth, but every one that believeth, now receiveth righteousness, in the full sense of that word; that is, he is justified, sanctified, and glorified... We are "dead to the law, by the body of Christ," given for us (Rom. 7:4), [and] God hath established another law in its place, even the law of faith. And we are all under this law to God and to Christ... Is love the fulfilling of this law? Unquestionably it is. The whole law, under which we now are, is fulfilled by love (Rom. 13:9, 10). Faith working or animated by love is all that God now requires of man... [This] love is the end of every commandment of God. It is the point aimed at by the whole and every part of the Christian institution... [It is] the loving the Lord our God with

---

[154] John Wesley, *Works [BE]*, Vol. 2, p.9.

[155] John Wesley, *Explanatory Notes upon The New Testament*, Gal. 3:24.

all our heart, mind, soul, and strength; and the loving our neighbour, every man, as ourselves, as our own souls.[156]

Wesley believed that he had now demonstrated from Scripture that the faith wrought in the Christian's heart by the Spirit so exercised and energised his whole soul that it resulted in the love of God and man. This was perfection, Christian perfection, and its description by Paul as 'faith working by love' (Gal. 5:6) became the most familiar Scripture text scattered throughout Wesley's writings. And his constant insistence that true faith produced holy, obedient love enabled him to rebut all forms of antinomianism. This emphasis on Christian holiness as perfected love was also important for his understanding of the nature of sin. While he frequently defined sin as 'the voluntary transgression of a known law,' his implications were often more scripturally sound than the bare meaning of the definition. The decade of the 1760's witnessed a lot of unrest in the Methodist Societies concerning this doctrine of Christian perfection. The defection of two of Wesley's preachers, Thomas Maxfield and George Bell, into extremes of perfectionist claims early in the decade, had given the doctrine a bad name and Wesley was forced to remove both men from the Connexion. He had compiled the, *Plain Account* to clarify his teaching on entire sanctification and at the same time he continued to answer questions from his Methodist people on the topics of temptation, sin and perfection. He assured Elizabeth Bennis that there is an important distinction between sins and infirmities. 'A thousand infirmities are consistent even with the highest degree of holiness, which is no other than pure love, an heart devoted to God, one design and one desire.'[157] Later he wrote to her. 'Nothing is sin, strictly speaking, but a voluntary transgression of a known law of God. Therefore every voluntary breach of the law of love is sin... There may be ten thousand wandering thoughts and forgetful intervals without any breach of love, though not without transgressing the Adamic law.'[158] This might be called Wesley's fuller definition of sin and,

[156] John Wesley, *Works*, Vol. 11, pp.415, 416.
[157] John Wesley, *Letters*, Vol. 5, p.6.
[158] John Wesley, *Letters*, Vol. 5, p.322.

significantly, it refers to any breach of 'the law of love.' In other places where Wesley spoke of sin as transgressing the law, it was the law of love he had in mind but he did not always spell it out fully. In the, *Plain Account*, he argued that Christians are not measured by the perfect law given to Adam in Eden, but rather by the law given in Christ's Great Commandment. 'You shalt love the Lord your God with all your heart... soul... mind... and... your neighbour as thyself' (Matt. 22:37-39). To love God and neighbour with all the heart is the fulfilling of the law; consequently, sin is any breach of this law of love. John Wesley believed that the entirely sanctified Christian was enabled by God's grace to love both God and his neighbour and such love is Christian perfection.

One of the criticisms most frequently made of Wesley's definition of sin as voluntary transgression is that it is not comprehensive enough. It fails to take account of sins of omission, that is, those actions in which the Christian fails to do the good that he might have done. In this way, it is argued, our sins of omission may be as serious as sins of commission, yet Wesley's definition fails to take account of them. But this criticism has not considered John Wesley's definition closely enough. In his letters to Elizabeth Bennis he spoke of trials. 'It is by these your faith is made perfect. You will find many things both in your heart and in your life contrary to the perfection of the Adamic law, but it does not follow that they are contrary to the law of love.'[159] This most certainly includes sins of omission, for the failure to do good is, by definition, a failure to love our neighbour with all our hearts. It must be admitted that in the other passages where John Wesley defined sin as transgression of the law, it would have been more satisfactory if he had added this fuller understanding of any breach of the law of love. Given the pre-eminence that a loving God and neighbour has in all his writings, there can be no doubt at all that this was clearly his intention. Any failure to love God or neighbour Wesley designated sin, and with this understanding of it, he saw Christian holiness or Christian perfection, as the perfect love of God in man.

---

[159] John Wesley, *Letters*, Vol. 5, p.315.

In the, *Plain Account,* John Wesley was careful to teach that there is no experience of sanctifying grace that dispenses with the Christian's constant need of Christ's work. The holiest of believers still need Christ as their Prophet, Priest and King.[160] As their Prophet, he is the light of the world, and only as they walk with him in unbroken fellowship do they walk in the light. Should he withdraw, nothing remains but darkness. Similarly he is their King, giving them his sanctifying grace moment by moment. Holiness is not a stock of grace given to the Christian on which he can draw whether or not he is in fellowship with Christ. 'They must receive,' said Wesley, 'a supply every moment,'[161] otherwise they have no holiness of their own efforts or spiritual achievements. Likewise the entirely sanctified Christian needs Christ as his Priest to make atonement for him, for even full obedience and holy love is acceptable to God only through the merits of His Son. When critics said that Wesley's doctrine prompted professors of perfect love to say they did not need Christ's atonement any longer, he protested that they confessed just the contrary. The language of their heart is:

Every moment, Lord, I want
The merit of thy death.[162]

It was important to understand in what sense the fully sanctified Christian needs the benefits of Christ's atonement constantly and unfailingly. It is not in the sense of needing to be reconciled to God anew, for the justified Christian is already reconciled to God. Nor are Christ's atoning merits needed to restore the favour of God, but rather to enable the believer to continue to enjoy God's favour. 'He does not procure pardon for them anew, but "ever liveth to make intercession for them," and "by one offering he hath perfected for ever them that are sanctified"' (Heb. 10:14).[163]

---

[160] John Wesley, *Works*, Vol. 11, p.417.
[161] John Wesley, *Works*, Vol. 11, p.417.
[162] John Wesley, *Works*, Vol. 11, p.443.
[163] John Wesley, *Works*, Vol. 11, p.418.

Another of the emphases made by Wesley in the, *Plain Account,* was that this grace of Christian holiness is both instantaneous and progressive in Christian experience. In reply to the question of whether or not all sin is cleansed from the Christian's heart before the hour of death, Wesley responded that it does not require forty Scripture passages to prove that in most instances all inner sin is dealt with over a long period of time. But there is a wide variety of experiences among the people of God and Christians should look to God in faith for this blessing *now*, rather than compare their experiences with others. When pressed on the point of instantaneous deliverance from sin, Wesley admitted that he thought the scriptures 'silent upon the subject, because the point is not determined, at least not in express terms, in any part of the oracles of God.'[164] The New Testament speaks of those who are now sanctified, and to this certainty Wesley added the many witnesses he believed he knew who were enjoying this 'full salvation' now. To this end he advised his Methodist preachers. 'All our preachers should make a point of preaching perfection to believers constantly, strongly and explicitly, and all believers should mind this one thing, and continually agonize for it.'[165] Even if the majority of Christians did not experience this full deliverance from sin until the moment before the soul leaves the body, yet equally it might be received ten, twenty or forty years before. Two other constants in Wesley's understanding of Christian perfection were dealt with in the, *Plain Account*; the witness of the Spirit to entire sanctification and regaining what had been lost. In 1763 Wesley published a tract entitled, *Farther Thoughts on Christian Perfection*. It was written specifically to give biblical and pastoral guidance to the increasing number of Methodists who were seeking and claiming the experience of perfect love. Written in the form of question and answer, Question 16 asked how the Christian could know that they were saved from 'inbred corruption.' Wesley's response was fairly predictable. As with justification, he argued for the inner testimony of the Spirit in holy living. He conceded that for both justification and entire sanctification, the inner witness of the Spirit

---

[164] John Wesley, *Works [BE],* Vol. 3, p.177.
[165] John Wesley, *Works*, Vol. 11, p.443.

may not come immediately to the obedient Christian, nor is it always strong and constant. Although he did not refer directly to Romans 8:16, it was clearly this passage that he had in mind. 'The same Spirit beareth witness with our spirits that we are the children of God.' This scripture is generally understood as referring to the Spirit bearing witness with the consciousness of the justified Christian and doesn't obviously refer to what Wesley understood as entire sanctification. A year earlier he had dealt with this assurance in a published sermon.

> What is that faith whereby we are sanctified? It is a divine evidence and conviction, first, that God hath promised it in the Holy Scripture... Secondly, that what God promised he is *able* to perform... Thirdly, that he is able and willing to do it *now*... To this confidence... there needs to be added one thing more; a divine evidence and conviction that he doth it. In that hour it is done. God says to the inmost soul, 'According to thy faith be it unto thee.' Then the soul is pure from every spot of sin.[166]

The sermon concludes with a searching appeal that the Christian must exercise faith at this very moment. 'Expect it by *faith*, expect it *as you are*, and expect it *now*!'[167] As always, John Wesley, the practical theologian, convinced that Scripture clearly promised full salvation from sin in this life, urged his converts to seek it *now* by faith. A command to be holy is a 'covered promise' that God both can and will make his people holy. God can do it, God will do it – and he will do it now. Wesley was far more concerned with helping the Methodists to experience what he called their 'grand depositum' than he was in multiplying arguments for its reality. It was promised, he believed, in scripture, and that was enough.

The decade of the 1760's had witnessed both an increasing number of Wesley' converts testifying their experience of entire sanctification and a marked increase in debates and controversies surrounding the teaching. At the pastoral level Wesley was well aware that many who professed this blessing of full sanctification later seemed to fall away

---

[166] John Wesley, *Works [BE],* Vol. 2, pp.167-168.
[167] John Wesley, *Works [BE],* Vol. 2, p.169.

from it. He needed to give advice on losing and reclaiming the grace of God. He wrote: 'We do not find any general state described in Scripture from which a man cannot draw back to sin... They who are sanctified may yet fall and perish.'[168] For that reason the Christian must always be watchful and heed the Johannine injunction, 'Love not the world.' Wesley then incorporated into the text of the, *Plain Account,* the directions he had published four years earlier under the title, *Cautions and Directions given to the Greatest Professors in the Methodist Societies*.[169] These consisted of seven admonitions on how to walk in the way of holy obedience. They included; watching and praying against pride, avoiding the Antinomian deception that Christians need no longer observe the moral law, watching against sins of omission by always doing good, and living the Christian life in what Wesley described as 'deep, steady seriousness.'[170] If, however, the Christian falls away from this grace of full salvation, the way of recovery is through confession repentance and faith. 'If any of you should fall from what you now are... do not deny, do not hide, do not disguise it at all, at the peril of your soul... Surely He will again lift up your head, and cause the bones that have been broken to rejoice.'[171]

The Doctrine's Biblical Foundations

If there was any one conviction that John Wesley held about the doctrine of Christian perfection that outweighed all others in his thinking, it was his certainty that this doctrine was taught in holy scripture. He constantly referred to it as 'scriptural holiness,' and near the end of the, *Plain Account,* he replied to the charge that he had invented this doctrine. 'I found it in the oracles of God, in the Old and New Testament... It is the doctrine of St. Paul, the doctrine of St. James,

[168] John Wesley, *Works*, Vol. 11, p.422.
[169] John Wesley had written and published this 12 page pamphlet as an antidote against the extravagant perfectionist claims of the expelled preachers, Thomas Maxfield and George Bell.
[170] John Wesley, *Works*, Vol. 11, pp.427-435.
[171] John Wesley, *Works*, Vol. 11, p.435.

of St. Peter, and St. John.'[172] He had prefaced the, *Plain Account,* by saying that in 1729 he had begun to study the Bible as against merely reading it, and there he saw, 'in a clearer light, the indispensable necessity of having "the mind which was in Christ"... of walking as he walked, not only in many, or in most respects, but in all things.'[173] While it is not possible in this analysis to attempt a systematic exegesis of all the biblical passages that John Wesley used in his explication of this doctrine, it is necessary to at least draw attention to those texts that he used most often. They are found mostly in the, *Plain Account*, and in the sermons dealing with Christian holiness. In all instances the texts will be cited as Wesley wrote them, which was, in the main, in the King James text but occasionally he made use of his own translation. This selection will deal only with those texts on which John Wesley made some exegetical commentary, as distinct from texts cited without comment. Also, the order of the texts will be the order found in Wesley's writings.

While the great majority of the biblical passages were taken from the New Testament, there were four Old Testament texts that he used frequently. He interpreted Deuteronomy 6:5 as a description of the perfect believer; loving God 'with all our heart, and mind, and soul.'[174] God's promise to take away inner sin was read in Ezekiel 36:29; 'saved from all our uncleannesses,' a promise which Wesley thought was as clear as any biblical promise could be.[175] It was reinforced by Psalm 130:8, 'He shall redeem Israel from all his sins.'[176] The language of symbolic circumcision in Deuteronomy 30:6 strengthened the use already made of Deuteronomy 6:5; 'The Lord God will circumcise thy heart... to love the Lord thy God with all thy heart and with all thy soul.'[177] Wesley found no difficulty in applying to Christian experience the words addressed to the whole nation of Israel under the old

[172] John Wesley, *Works*, Vol. 11, p.444.
[173] John Wesley, *Works,* Vol. 11, p.367.
[174] John Wesley, *Works*, Vol. 11, p.387.
[175] John Wesley, *Works*, Vol. 11, p.387.
[176] John Wesley, *Works*, Vol. 11, p.389.
[177] John Wesley, *Works*, Vol. 11, p.389.

covenant. Neither God's call to his people to be holy, nor his promises to make them holy, can be denied, so texts from the Torah, the Prophets or the Psalms, apply to Christians as fully as they did to believing Israelites.

Answering these Old Testament promises in 'the plainest terms' are the words of 1 John 3:8. 'For this purpose the Son of God was manifested that he might destroy the works of the devil.' Since all sin is the work of the devil this can mean no less than a promise of the end of sin. Likewise in Ephesians 5:25-27. 'Christ loved the Church and gave himself for it... that it might be holy and without blemish.'[178] Romans 8:3-4 is read to the same end, that the righteousness of the law might be fulfilled in us, who walk not after the flesh, but after the spirit.'[179] There are also prayers in the New Testament for believers and they contain petitions for deliverance from sin and establishment in grace. To this end Jesus taught his disciples to pray, 'Deliver us from evil,' and he prayed for them, 'I in them and thou in me, that they may be made perfect in one' (Lk. 11:4; Jn. 17:23). Paul prayed that the Ephesian Christians might be 'filled with all the fullness of God' and for the Thessalonian believers that God would sanctify them 'wholly' (Eph. 3:19; 1 Thess. 5:23).

As well as New Testament prayers for holiness, there are also commands that God's people should be holy. Jesus commanded, 'Be ye perfect, as your Father who is in heaven is perfect' (Matt. 5:48). In his, *Explanatory Notes*, Wesley translated, 'Therefore ye shall be perfect, as your father....' He added, 'So the original implies, referring to all that holiness, which our Lord in the beginning of the chapter recommends as happiness, and in the close of it as perfection.'[180] He found another command to holiness in the 'Great Commandment' of Matthew 22:37-40, one of his favourite passages in his promotion of scriptural holiness. 'Thou shall love the Lord thy God with all thy heart, and with all thy soul, and with all thy mind.' He reasoned from

---

[178] John Wesley, *Works*, Vol. 11, p.389.
[179] John Wesley, *Works,* Vol. 11, p.389.
[180] John Wesley, *Explanatory Notes upon The New Testament, Matt*. 5:48.

this command that 'if the love of God fill all the heart, there can be no sin therein.'[181] This exegetical note is an example of how John Wesley understood Christian holiness, especially from the 1760's onwards, increasingly in terms of 'love excluding sin.'

Of particular importance for Wesley's doctrine of deliverance from sin were Paul's words in Romans 13:9, 'Love is the fulfilling of the law.' In this Christian dispensation, all believers are bound by the law of faith which requires them to love God and their neighbour. In this way love 'fulfils' the law. Wesley reasoned: 'The whole law under which we now are, is fulfilled by love (Rom. xiii. 9, 10). Faith working or animated by love is all that God now requires. He has substituted (not sincerity, but) love, in the room of angelic perfection.'[182] In this context Paul's declaration that 'love is the end of the commandment' (1 Tim. 1:5), is interpreted in line with the words in Romans 13. 'Love is the end of every commandment of God. It is the point aimed at by the whole and every part of the Christian institution. The foundation is faith, purifying the heart; the end love, preserving a good conscience.'[183] This means loving the Lord our God with all our heart, loving our neighbour 'as ourselves, as our own souls,' and the 'fruits' of this love are seen in Paul's delineation of the Christ-like character in 1 Corinthians 13.

John Wesley read Hebrews 6:1 as proof that perfection, understood as cleansing from sin and loving God with all the heart, is an experience of grace subsequent to justification. The words, 'let us go on to perfection' are an exhortation to Christians and must therefore point beyond Christian initiation.[184] Although he contented himself with this

---

[181] John Wesley, *Works*, Vol. 11, p.390.

[182] John Wesley, *Works*, Vol. 11, p.416. Commenting on Paul's words, 'Owe no man any thing but to love one another: for he that loveth another hath fulfilled the law,' Wesley reasoned, 'To love one another. An eternal debt which can never be sufficiently discharged. But yet if this be rightly performed, it discharges all the rest... So that if you were not thinking of it, yet if your heart was full of love, you would fulfil it.'

[183] John Wesley, *Works*, Vol. 11, p.416.

[184] John Wesley, *Works*, Vol. 11, p.441.

brief comment on the text in the, *Plain Account*, it was also the text for his 1784 sermon, *On Perfection.* He defined 'perfection' as 'this mind which also in Christ Jesus' (Phil. 2:5), which 'includes the whole disposition of his mind, all his affections, all his tempers, both toward God and man. Now it is certain that as there was no evil affection in him, so no good affection or temper was wanting.'[185] This is the 'perfection' to which every Christian must 'go on.' Another fitting description is 'the one undivided fruit of the Spirit' adumbrated in Galations 5:22, 23. Again it means putting on 'the new man which is created after God in righteousness and true holiness' (Eph. 4:24), or as Peter spoke of it, 'As he that hath called you is holy, so be ye holy in all manner of conversation' (1 Pet. 1:15). From the use of the term 'perfection' in Hebrews 6:1 and the interpretation Wesley gave to the other scriptural passages he selected, he concluded, 'Perfection is another name for universal holiness – inward and outward righteousness – holiness of life arising from holiness of heart.'[186]
John Wesley drew attention to the important uses of the word 'perfect' in Philippians 3, verses 12 and 15. He translated the former ('not as though I... were already perfect') as 'or am already perfected' and the latter as, 'Let us, as many as are perfect.' He commented, 'There is a difference between one that is perfect [i.e. v.15] and one that is perfected [i.e. v.12]. The one is fitted for the race, v.15; the other, ready to receive the prize.'[187] In the, *Plain Account*, the 'perfection' of v.15 is spoken of as Christian experience which is not 'so late as death, for St. Paul speaks of living men that were perfect.'[188] In his 1741 sermon, *Christian Perfection,* Wesley attempted to 'remove the difficulty arising from this seeming contradiction' between verses 12 and 15. The 'perfection' which Paul disclaims in the former verse Wesley explained, as he would consistently do throughout his ministry, as any notion of perfection that meant entire deliverance from ignorance, errors of judgement, infirmities and temptation. Such perfection does not belong to our present pilgrimage. Wesley then defined the

---

185 John Wesley, *Works [BE],* Vol. 3, p.74.
186 John Wesley, *Works [BE],* Vol. 3, p.75.
187 John Wesley, *Explanatory Notes upon the New Testament*, Phil. 3:12-15.
188 John Wesley, *Works*, Vol. 11, p.442.

perfection claimed by Paul in v.15. 'In conformity both to the doctrine of St. John, and to the whole tenor of the new Testament, we fix this conclusion: "A Christian is so far perfect as not to commit sin."'[189]

One other Pauline passage that Wesley employed in his exposition of Christian perfection was Galations 2:19, 20. 'For I through the law am dead to the law, that I may live to God. I am crucified with Christ, and I live not longer but Christ liveth in me...' He explained Paul's claim.

> The apostle describes how he is free, how far he is from continuing therein. Every real Christian can say with St. Paul, 'I am crucified with Christ: nevertheless I live; yet not I, but Christ liveth in me' – words that manifestly describe a deliverance from inward as well as outward sin. This is expressed both negatively, 'I live not' – my evil nature, the body of sin, is destroyed – and positively, 'Christ liveth in me' – and therefore all that is holy, and just, and good.[190]

John Wesley found a number of passages in 1 John that he quoted and explained many times in his defence of sanctification as deliverance from sin and perfection in love. When John spoke of 'perfect love' (4:18), Wesley took these words to mean the very essence of Christian perfection. 'The natural man, this is, the man who has not yet responded to prevenient grace, has neither fear or love; the awakened man has fear without love; the newly-justified Christian experiences love and fear, but a father in Christ', a mature and fully sanctified Christian, enjoys 'love without fear.'[191] The Apostle's promise that 'the blood of Jesus Christ his Son cleanseth us from all sin' (1 Jn. 1:7), points indisputably to present Christian experience.

> It is evident the Apostle here speaks of a deliverance wrought in this world: For he saith not, The blood of Christ will cleanse (at the hour of death, or in the day of judgement), but it

---

[189] John Wesley, *Works [BE],* Vol. 2, p.116. In the pages preceding this conclusion, Wesley argued for sin to be understood as a wilful breaking of God's commandments; i.e. deliberate and intentional transgression.

[190] John Wesley, *Explanatory Notes upon The New Testament*, Gal. 2:20. *Works [BE],* Vol. 2, p.118.

[191] John Wesley, *Explanatory Notes upon The New Testament*, 1 Jn. 4:18.

> 'cleanseth,' at the time present, us living Christians 'from all sin.' And it is equally evident, that if any sin remain, we are not cleansed from 'all' sin... It remains then, that Christians are saved in this world from all sin, from all unrighteousness.[192]

Wesley saw no contradiction between the promise of full cleansing from all sin promised in v.7 with the warnings expressed in the verses following. 'If we say we have no sin we deceive ourselves,' and, 'If we say we have not sinned, we make him a liar.' Our 'having no sin' and our 'having not sinned' concern what we were before we experienced God's saving and cleansing grace. No man or woman can truthfully refuse the offer of God's forgiving grace by claiming either, 'I have no sin,' or, 'I have not sinned.' All human beings have sinned and all need the forgiveness of sins and the cleansing from unrighteousness promised in v.9. To deny this is to make God a liar. When the sinner confesses his sin, God not only grants him forgiveness of sins but also cleansing from all unrighteousness that he may 'go and sin no more.'[193]

From as early as 1741 John Wesley used 1 John 3:8,9, in defence of his teaching that a true Christian can be delivered in this life from wilful sinning. 'The Son of God was manifested to destroy the works of the devil. Whosoever is born of God doth not commit sin; for his seed abideth in him, and he cannot sin, because he is born of God.' The work of was Christ to destroy sin and Wesley argued that this means dethroning sin in the human heart and then extirpating it. Here in this plain Johannine statement, he believed, was clear proof that Christ could deal effectively with all our sin. For the man or woman who is truly 'born of God,' committing sin is a moral impossibility. Such is the moment by moment communion between the regenerated soul and Christ that sin, understood as a voluntary breaking of any of God's commandment, is a moral impossibility. Wesley argued:

> 'Whosoever is born of God, while he abideth in faith and love, and in the spirit of prayer and thanksgiving, not only doth not, but cannot, thus commit sin. So long as he thus believeth in God

---

[192] John Wesley, *Works*, Vol. 11, pp.377, 378.
[193] John Wesley, *Works*, Vol. 11, p.376.

> through Christ, and loves him, and is pouring out his heart before him, he cannot voluntarily transgress any command of God, either by speaking or acting what he knows God hath forbidden: So long that seed which remaineth in him, that loving, praying, thankful faith, compels him to refrain from whatsoever he knows to be an abomination in the sight of God.[194]

John Wesley knew, however, that Christian experience could not deny the plain fact that many of those who are truly born of God do, in fact, commit sin. How does this unquestionable conclusion square with John's insistence that those born of God 'cannot' sin? Wesley reasoned that this is because the Christian does not respond to the Holy Spirit who is warning him of the temptation to which he is attracted.

> A temptation arises, whether from the world, the flesh or the devil, it matters not. The Spirit of God gives him warning that sin is near, and bids him more abundantly watch unto prayer. He gives way, in some degree, to the temptation, which now begins to grow pleasing to him. The Holy Spirit is grieved; his faith is weakened, and his love to God grows cold. The Spirit reproves him more sharply, and saith, 'This is the way; walk thou in it. He turns away from the painful voice of God, and listens to the pleasing voice of the tempter. Evil desire begins and spreads in his soul, till faith and love vanish away: He is then capable of committing outward sin, the power of the Lord being departed from him.[195]

In this way Wesley understood that being born of God means that God is ever breathing into the Christian's soul the inspiration of His Spirit and the Christian responds by continually offering up all his thoughts and words and actions to God. While this unbroken communion continues, the Christian 'cannot' disobey his Lord whom he loves with all his heart and soul and mind. This is the essence of Christian perfection.

---

[194] John Wesley, *Works [BE],* Vol. 1, p.436.
[195] John Wesley, *Works [BE],* Vol. 1, p.440.

As with the other doctrines of the faith, John Wesley employed the Scriptures in a 'proof texting' way to expound his doctrine of Christian perfection. Convinced that all Scripture is God's word and that it is to be understood in its plain, literal meaning, he freely quoted texts from both Testaments that served his purpose. A promise to Israel that God would cleanse the nation from spiritual idolatry is a promise that the New Testament Christian can be cleansed from all inner sin. Texts that promise cleansing, sanctification and deliverance from sin, wherever found, are texts that the Christian can rely on. When he was half persuaded to drop the controversial perfectionist terminology, he returned to it for the simple reason that it was 'in the Bible.' If a particular text does not fully support the weight of interpretation that Wesley gives to it, his reply is that his interpretation is valid because it is in line with 'the whole tenor of Scripture.'

Did John Wesley's exposition of selected biblical texts demonstrate that his interpretation of Christian perfection has a *scriptural* foundation? The answer to that question is a qualified yes. Wesley was able to claim that in this Christian dispensation God calls his redeemed people to holy living. The New Testament teaching on justification and sanctification is to the end, 'Be holy, for I am holy.' Through the redemptive work of Christ and the sanctifying ministry of the holy Spirit, God both wills and enables his people to be holy. It is the 'pure in heart' who see God and there is abundant evidence in the New Testament that Christians are called to be like their Lord in holy conduct. John Wesley's insistence in this connection was right; he knew that the Scriptures called believers to Christ-likeness. His distinctive emphases on entire sanctification, however, are not so convincingly demonstrated by his use of Scripture. His insistence on the instantaneous nature of full sanctification is not proven by his exegeses, neither is his fairly constant emphasis that it must be consequent to justification. His use of perfectionist terminology was problematic, though he was undoubtedly close to New Testament teaching when he interpreted perfection in terms of love to God and man. Our Lord's 'Great Commandment,' to all his people, 'You shall love the Lord your God with all your heart... and your neighbour as yourself...' expressed the standard of holy conduct by which all Christians must measure themselves. Whatever it lacks in terms of precise biblical and theological formulation, John Wesley's doctrine of Christian holiness was an attempt both to interpret our Lord's teaching and encourage all believers to seek its practical implementation in their lives.

LECTURE 4
JOHN WESLEY AND EVANGELISM

Two-hundred-and-thirty-two years ago, on Wednesday, March 2, 1791, John Wesley died in London. By any measure his was a remarkable life. It spanned almost the whole of the eighteenth-century, from 1703 to 1791, and it witnessed sixty years of preaching, fifty of which were mostly occupied with itinerant evangelism, in what Wesley himself called 'field preaching'. That open-air preaching began in a brickyard in Bristol on Monday April 2, 1739, and it finished under an ash tree in Winchelsea, Sussex, on Thursday, October 7, 1790. Wesley's sermon text in Bristol was from Luke 4. 'The Spirit of the Lord is upon me, because He has anointed me to preach good news...' The text for his final sermon out of doors was Mark 1:15. 'Repent and believe the gospel.' This lecture will examine how Wesley's preaching ministry began, how he understood evangelism, and the nature of the institutions he created for the consolidation and continuance of the work.

Three particular years in John Wesley's life stand out with special significance; 1725, 1738 and 1739. In 1725 Wesley believed he was called of God to enter 'holy orders,' i.e. ordination in the Church of England. He prepared for this service and what it entailed with scrupulous self-examination.

> In the year 1725, being in the twenty-third year of my age, I met with Bishop Taylor's "Rule and Exercises of Holy Living and Dying."--- I was exceedingly affected; that part in particular which relates to purity of intention. Instantly I resolved to dedicate all my life to God, all my thoughts, and words, and actions. --- In the year 1726 I met with Kempis's "Christian's Patter." The nature and extent of inward religion, the religion of the heart, now appeared to me in a stronger light than ever it had done before. --- A year or two after, Mr. Law's "Christian Perfection" and "Serious Call" were put into my hands. These convinced me, more than ever, of the absolute impossibility of being half a Christian, and I determined,

through his grace --- to be all-devoted to God, to give him all my soul, body, and my substance.[196]

While it could not be described as an evangelical conversion, this choice to become a preacher affected Wesley for the rest of his life. Just how seriously he took his ordination as a deacon, and later his vows as a priest in 1728, is illustrated by a letter he wrote many years later to his brother Charles. 'Your business, as well as mine, is to save souls. When he took priests' orders, we undertook to make it our one business. I think every day lost which is not (mainly at least) employed in this thing.'[197] As to why John Wesley decided to become a preacher, the answer is because it was in his blood. His father, Samuel Wesley, his grandfather, John Wesley, and his great-grandfather, Bartholomew Wesley, were all preachers of the gospel. On the maternal side, his mother Susanna was the daughter of London's celebrated Puritan preacher, Samuel Annesley. Wesley once remarked that it was a sequence almost unknown in English Church history that four generations of the same family had all been gospel preachers. Although there is no doubt that he thought he had a very clear and definite call from God to be a preacher, Wesley could not possibly have foreseen the kind of ministry that the Lord of the Church was preparing him for.

Early in 1738 John Wesley returned home to England from Georgia. On the outward journey he had made friends with Moravian families also bound for Georgia. For the next two years Wesley was deeply impressed with the spiritual calibre of the Moravians and particularly their emphasis on justification by faith that brought the assurance of sins forgiven and peace with God. Between February and May 1738, both John and Charles Wesley were in close contact with another Moravian, Peter Bohler, and he played a very large part in the events of Pentecost 1738. On that Sunday, Charles professed personal saving

---

[196] John Wesley, *Works*, Vol. 11, pp.366, 367.
[197] John Wesley, *Works*, Vol. 12, p.139.

faith, as John did the following Wednesday evening.[198] In both their experiences the sense of personal assurance was very prominent, as it would be in their subsequent preaching. Following his 'heart-warming' experience, and after visiting the Moravian headquarters in Saxony, Germany, John Wesley continued to preach the doctrine of justification by faith he had learned more fully from his Moravian contacts. Most of this preaching was in the London area, in meetings of the Religious Societies, in Moravian gatherings and in private homes. From about mid-September 1738 onwards, there are detailed references in John Wesley's *Journal* to his almost daily preaching the gospel of salvation by faith. The entries also include hints that his preaching was not always warmly received by the parish clergy. 'I was enabled to speak strong words at St. Anne's, and twice at St. John's, Clerkenwell, so that I fear they will bear me there no longer.' 'I preached to such a congregation as I never saw before at St. Clement's in the Strand. As this was the first time of my preaching here, I suppose it is to be the last' 'I preached at St. Giles... How the power of God was present with us! I am content to preach here no more.'[199]

Wesley was well aware that the reason for his exclusion from Church of England pulpits was because his 'new' doctrine of salvation by faith was ridiculed as 'enthusiasm,' that is, fanaticism, by most of the clergy. Writing a few years later in his, *A Farther Appeal to Men of Reason and Religion*,' he explained what happened.

> Whenever I was now desired to preach, salvation by faith was my only theme. My constant subjects were, 'Believe in the Lord Jesus Christ, and thou shalt be saved.' 'Him hath God exalted to be a Prince and a Saviour, to give repentance and remission of sins.' These I explained and enforced with all my might, in every church where I was asked to preach... Things were in this posture, when I was told I must preach no more in this, and this, and another church; the reason was usually

[198] Charles Wesley, *The Journal of Charles Wesley*, Vol. 1, pp.90-92. John Wesley, *Works [BE],* Vol. 18, pp.249, 250.

[199] John Wesley, *Works [BE],* Vol. 19, p.13.

> added without reserve, 'Bccause you preach such doctrines.'[200]

By 'such doctrines' Wesley meant justification by faith and the witness of the Spirit to personal forgiveness and acceptance. He added that he was forbidden 'as by a general consent, to preach in any church (though not by any judicial sentence) for preaching such doctrine. This was the open, avowed cause.'[201] Nearly twenty years later he outlined in a letter to a clerical friend the same reasons for his expulsion.

> The reproach of Christ arose first when my brother and I were at Oxford, from our endeavouring to be real Christians. It was abundantly increased when we began to preach repentance and remission of sins, and insist that we are justified by faith. For this cause were we excluded from preaching in the churches. I say for *this*: as yet there was no field preaching. And this exclusion occasioned our preaching elsewhere, with the other irregularities that followed.[202]

Wesley was in no doubt that it was for preaching justification by faith that he was excluded from the pulpits of the Church of England in 1739 onwards. This doctrine, learned from the formularies of his church but greatly enhanced and focused by his Moravian contacts, was the 'heart' of his evangel from May 1738 onwards. It was this emphasis on justification by faith that Wesley acknowledged as the reason for the growing success of his ministry post 1738. In a long apologia penned in 1746, he reviewed his preaching from 1725 onwards and made his discovery of justification by faith the reason for his increasing effectiveness.

> From the year 1725 to 1729 I preached much, but saw no fruit to my labour. Indeed it could not be that I should; for I neither laid the foundation of repentance, nor of believing the gospel.... From the year 1729 to 1734, laying a deeper foundation of repentance, I saw a little fruit. But it was only a little; and no wonder: For I did not preach faith in the blood of the covenant.

---

200 John Wesley, *Works [BE],* Vol. 11, p.177.

201 John Wesley, *Works [BE],* Vol. 11, p.178.

202 John Wesley, *Letters*, Vol. 3, p.225.

> From 1734 to 1738, speaking more of faith in Christ, I saw more fruit of my preaching.... From 1738 to this time, speaking continually of Jesus Christ, laying him only for the foundation of the whole building.... The word of God ran as fire among stubble.... multitudes crying out, 'What must I do to be saved?'[203]

There is, then, the clearest evidence, that something happened to John Wesley in 1738 that changed his own spiritual experience and the thrust and power of his preaching. However the events of the evening of May 24, 1738, are explained in terms of his relationship with God, they gave him not only a new sense of acceptance with God and deep inner peace, but they also made him an evangelist. Henry Bett described it well in terms of a new manifestation of the power of the Holy Spirit in his life and ministry.

> He never feared death again in any of the perils or sickness of his life, from the day that he "felt his heart strangely warmed" to the day, more than fifty years later, when he died with words of triumph on his lips, "The best of all is, God is with us." And there had come to him also a spiritual energy, an evangelical zeal, an unction of the Holy One, that he had never before possessed. That hour in Aldersgate Street was the real beginning of his unique apostolate... with an assurance and a power and a peace and a joy he had never known before.[204]

By the end of 1738, John Wesley, with his 'warm heart' experience and his deep commitment to the doctrine of justification by faith, was equipped to be an effective evangelist. Although the churches were closing their doors to him, the Religious Societies gave him daily opportunities to exercise his preaching ministry and already there were signs of the larger harvest that would follow. When he returned home from Hernhut, he brought papers, which he intended to translate into English, but the demands made on him by preaching gave him no time for other work. 'It has pleased God to give me full employment of another nature. His blessed Spirit has wrought so powerfully, both in

---

[203] John Wesley, *Works,* Vol. 8, pp.468, 469.
[204] Henry Bett, *The Spirit of Methodism*, pp.35-37.

London and Oxford, that there is a general awakening and multitudes are crying out, "What must I do to be saved?"'[205] A month later he wrote likewise. 'Even to this hour I have not had one day's leisure to transcribe for you the papers I brought from Hernhut. The harvest here also is so plenteous, and the labourers so few, and it increases upon us daily. Verily the 'spirit of the Lord hath lift up his standard against the iniquity which had overspread our land as a flood."'[206] Three months later, in a letter to George Whitefield, Wesley continues to speak of how he is fully occupied with preaching and evangelism and of how the blessings of God attend his ministry. 'Our Lord's hand is not shortened among us. Yesterday I preached at St. Katherine's and at Islington.... And the fields after service were white with people praising God. About three hundred were present at Mr. Sim's.... At the Savoy on Thursday evening we have usually two or three hundred.... Mr. Abbot's parlour is more than filled on Friday.'[207]

John Wesley and George Whitefield were in regular correspondence with each other at this time, mostly reporting on their evangelistic endeavours. In February 1739 Whitefield took on a new ministry – preaching out-of-doors. In Kingswood in Bristol, he was challenged by the large number of people unreached with the gospel, people who were not disposed to attend any church services. Whitefield was determined to take the gospel to them and on Saturday afternoon, February 17, the die was truly cast. The Revd. George Whitefield, former member of the Oxford 'Holy Club,' now twenty five years old and an ordained minister in the Established Church, preached the gospel under the open skies for the first time. Standing on a hill in Kingswood, he preached to about two hundred miners, and recorded: 'Blessed be God that I have now broken the ice. I believe I was never more acceptable to my Master than when I was standing to teach those hearers in the open fields. Some may censure me, but if thus pleased men I should not be the servant of Christ.'[208] Soon Whitefield's open-

---

[205] John Wesley, *Works [BE],* Vol. 25, p.568.
[206] John Wesley, *Works [BE],* Vol. 25, pp.582, 583.
[207] John Wesley, *Works [BE],* Vol. 25, pp. 601, 602.
[208] George Whitefield, Vol. 1, p.256.

air congregations were numbered in thousands and he wrote of how the fire is kindled in the country. 'Preached at Hanham to a larger congregation than ever, and again in the afternoon to upwards of 25,000 people. I was afterwards told that those who stood farthest off could hear me plainly. Oh, may God speak to them by His Spirit, at the same time that He enables me to lift up my voice like a trumpet.'[209]

This amazing ministry grew daily and toward the end of March that year, Whitefield, planning to go to America, invited John Wesley to come to Bristol. 'I wish you would be here the latter end of next week... Come, I beseech you, come quickly. I have promised not to leave this people until you or somebody else came to supply my place. --- I pray for a blessing on your journey, and in our meetings. The people expect you much. Though you come after, I heartily wish you may be preferred before me. Even so, Lord Jesus, Amen.--- The Lord direct us all in all things.'[210] When Wesley received Whitefield's letter in London, his first response was to decline, arguing that the London work demanded his time and attention. When he consulted the Scriptures by opening them at random, they seemed to confirm his hesitance. For twelve days he discussed the invitation with his friends, especially the Moravians, but they could not agree on the matter. His brother Charles was decisively against his going to Bristol. When the matter could not be solved by discussion, the group resorted to a typical Moravian expedient – they cast lots. The outcome was that John Wesley should go to Bristol. This important turning point in Wesley's life seems to have been reached by a strange process of events. As Skevington Wood observed.

> In the end the question was settled by sacred lot. The outcome was that Wesley left for Bristol, and entered as he himself said on 'a new period'[211] in his life. It was not what he would have decided if left to his own devices. It was not the unanimous choice of his Christian friends. It was the result of what the

---

[209] George Whitefield, Vol. 1, p.267.

[210] George Whitefield, Vol. 1, p.272.

[211] John Wesley, *Works [BE]*, Vol. 19, p.38.

> world would call chance. But who can doubt that God was in it?'[212]

Wesley arrived in Bristol on Saturday, March 31, 1739. He heard Whitefield preach at the Weaver's Hall and the two men conversed late into the night. There can be little doubt that Whitefield's 'field preaching' was a major point in their discussions. So far all John Wesley's preaching had been in churches, society meeting rooms and private homes but he was about to be exposed to the ministry that Whitefield had recently pioneered. The next day Wesley accompanied Whitefield and heard him preach three times out-of-doors. He confessed candidly: 'I could scarce reconcile myself at first to this strange way of preaching in the fields... having been all my life (till very lately) so tenacious of every point relating to decency and order, that I should have thought the saving of souls almost a sin if it had not been done in a church.'[213] On the Sunday evening he preached to the society meeting in Nicholas Street, and noted wryly that the chosen text, from the Sermon on the Mount, was 'one pretty remarkable precedent of field preaching.'

The next day, Monday, April 2, 1739, must be set down beside John Wesley's account of what happened to him on Wednesday, May 24, the previous year. The later account recorded the evangelical 'heart-warming' while the former related how his ecclesiastical Rubicon was crossed.

> At four in the afternoon I submitted to 'be more vile,' and proclaimed in the highways the glad tidings of salvation, speaking from a little eminence in a ground adjoining the city, to about three thousand people. The Scripture on which I spoke was this, 'The Spirit of the Lord is upon me, because he hath anointed me to preach the gospel to the poor. He hath sent me to heal the broken-hearted, to preach deliverance to the captives and recovery of sight to the blind, to set at liberty them that are bruised, to proclaim the acceptable year of the Lord.'[214]

---

[212] Arthur Wood, *The Burning Heart*, p.92.
[213] John Wesley, *Works [BE],* Vol. 19, p.46.
[214] John Wesley, *Works [BE],* Vol. 19, p.46.

Various years can be suggested for the beginnings of 'Methodism,' including John Wesley's choice of 1729, and also 1738, in connection with May 24 that year. The happenings of April 2, 1739 were certainly another landmark in the revival movement. Whatever hesitations were in Wesley's mind about Whitefield's 'unorthodox' methods, he nevertheless followed in his younger friend's footsteps and launched himself into half a century of itinerant evangelism. In the months between May 1738 and March 1739, there is quite a number of entries in John Wesley's *Journal* that indicate the doubts and fears and negative introspection that frequently troubled him. What is surely significant is that following his preaching at Bristol in April 1739, such entries almost disappear entirely from his journals and letters. He had found his life's work, perhaps it would not be too much to call it his destiny, at Bristol, and he gave the next fifty years to it with a passion and dedication that marked him out as the organiser and charismatic leader of England's 18th century Awakening. Beginning in the year 1737 and culminating in May 1738, John Wesley 'discovered' the heart of the gospel – justification by faith. On that eventful Wednesday evening in Aldersgate Street he found the personal assurance of peace with God and began to preach salvation by faith with a new-found power and conviction. That would be his theme for the next half century. The evangelist had found the evangel, and in the brickyard in Bristol, in April 1739, he found his congregation.

For the next three years most of John Wesley's itinerant ministry was confined to the two main centres of London and Bristol and the towns and villages that lay between them. He also preached in Wales in support of Howell Harris who was following a ministry of preaching and organising Societies in Wales very similar to what both John and Charles Wesley were doing. The number of converts was growing rapidly, especially in London and Bristol, and the latter city was the site of the first building erected by the new movement. The foundation stone of Methodism's first 'preaching house,' called the New Room, was laid in the Horse Fair early in May 1739. Many more Methodist buildings would be built in the coming years, and all of them were called 'preaching houses.' To have referred to them as 'churches' would have brought the charge that the Methodists were organising a new religious denomination and Wesley was determined this would not happen. Neither would he designate the buildings as 'chapels' for that would have caused the Methodists to be labelled Dissenters, another identification Wesley was very anxious to avoid. Later in 1739 a theological dispute among the members of the Fetter Lane Society in London led Wesley and his supporters to separate from them. A former cannon factory was purchased and Wesley set up his centre at the Foundery, which remained the London headquarters of Methodism until 1778.

Apart from some preaching visits to the Midlands, John Wesley's ministry was confined to the south and west of England until the summer of 1742. In May that year, at the suggestion of Lady Huntingdon, John Wesley, accompanied by one of her assistants, John Taylor, visited Newcastle-upon-Tyne. What happened in Newcastle is of great interest, on two accounts. First, it was the beginning of John Wesley's wider evangelistic ministry that would take him too so many places in Britain in the next forty nine years. It would include twenty two visits to Scotland, twenty one to Ireland, and an almost non-stop itinerary of England and visits to Wales. The other interest of the Newcastle visit was that it witnessed the kind of evangelism and subsequent follow-up care of the converts that would be the mark of John Wesley's 'Methodism' across the four kingdoms.

John Wesley arrived in Newcastle on Friday, May 28, 1742, and noted not only the drunkenness of many of its inhabitants but the swearing and cursing he heard even on the lips of children. 'Surely this place,' he wrote, 'is ripe for Him who "came not to call the righteous, but sinners to repentance."'[215] At seven on Sunday morning Wesley and Taylor stood at the Sandgate and began to sing the Hundredth Psalm. Three or four people gathered around out of curiosity and after some time the crowd had grown to three or four hundred. Wesley's sermon, based on Isaiah's words, "He was wounded for our transgressions...,"

---

[215] John Wesley, *Works [BE],* Vol. 19, p.268.

was a direct appeal to his hearers to see Christ crucified for them. Wesley gives us no more information about the content of his first sermon in Newcastle but it should be noted that this Isaianic text was one of a number he used many times in his field preaching. As he preached the numbers grew to something like twelve to fifteen hundred people, who stood staring at him with amazement. He told them, 'If you desire to know who I am, my name is John Wesley. At five in the evening, with God's help, I design to preach here again.'[216]

When Wesley returned in the evening he found the hill covered with such a gathering of people that he reckoned the number larger than anything he had witnessed at the two main preaching sites in London, Moorfields and Kennington Common. The sermon was based on Hosea's words, 'I will heal their backsliding and love them freely.' Wesley notes that when he had finished preaching, the poor people were 'ready to tread me under-foot, out of pure love and kindness.'[217] They followed him to his lodgings and implored him to stay longer but he and Taylor had promised to be in Yorkshire two days later.

John Wesley's preaching on this first visit to Newcastle, and what happened on subsequent visits, is a kind of model of the evangelism he pursued for the rest of his life. He began by preaching in the street and this was novel enough to attract a few curious people. After a while some more people gathered and Wesley preached to them, the Bible in one hand and the other raised often in the manner of public orators. From the eye-witness accounts that exist of Wesley's preaching, there is the general consensus that he had the ability to hold people's attention, even out-of-doors and with all the distractions that open-air preaching is exposed to. Attention will be given later to the important difference between the kind of sermons that Wesley preached in the streets of Newcastle and elsewhere throughout the country and the sermons he carefully prepared for publication. It is clear that these Newcastle sermons were meant to bring his congregation to the

---

216 John Wesley, *Works [BE],* Vol. 19, p.269.
217 John Wesley, *Works [BE],* Vol. 19, p.269.

experience of saving faith. Quite often the preaching was followed immediately by prayer, and then there was individual counselling and exhortation for those openly seeking the way of salvation. Although Wesley's first visit to Newcastle lasted only a few days, he was back there again seven months later. He made a third visit three months later, staying six weeks, and his record of what happened shows that the work there had been steadily growing in the intervening months. A 'Society' had been formed to bring together those spiritually awakened and Wesley spent a week meeting with the members and administering discipline, counsel and pastoral care. He removed the names of fifty people from the Society's roll who were not walking 'according to the gospel,' and he noted in his *Journal* that this left some eight hundred in the Society. The number of converts in Newcastle had been steadily growing since Wesley's first visit and eventually this centre would become his headquarters in the north-east of England.

Three years earlier, John and Charles had organised their followers in London into what were named 'United Societies,' and these societies were also set up in Bristol and the other places where the Wesleys had been preaching. The 'Bands,' consisting of small groups of five or six people meeting regularly for spiritual edification and to 'watch over each other's souls,' had been early instituted, following the example of the Moravians. When the 'New Room' was built in Bristol in 1739, it was suggested that the building could be paid for if all the members would agree to contribute a penny a week. The membership was divided into groups of twelve and the appointed leader was responsible for collecting the weekly contributions. But this organisation was to have spectacular consequences. The groups set up for the purpose of collecting money very quickly became gatherings for spiritual edification and very soon named 'Classes.' In this way the 'Methodist Class Meeting' came into being, arguably the most important and most successful of all the institutions of 18th century Methodists.

In Newcastle in February 1743, John Wesley wrote and published, *The Nature, Design, and General Rules of the United Societies, in London,*

Bristol, Kingswood and Newcastle-upon-Tyne.[218] He briefly outlined how the Societies came into being and then drew up guidelines for the Leaders, the conditions of membership and the kind of conduct expected from all the members. The membership conditions were simple. 'A desire to flee from the wrath to come, to be saved from all sins.' Would-be members were not required to be regenerate believers already. Membership was open to all those who sincerely *desired* to be Christians. The ethical requirements for membership were under three headings. First, a deliberate turning away from evil of every kind, including swearing, profaning the Lord's day, drunkenness and dealing in 'uncustomed' goods. Secondly, by 'doing good of every possible sort and as far as is possible to all men.' Thirdly, regular attendance at 'all the ordinances of God.' This meant that Wesley expected his people to be in regular attendance at their parish church as well as the means of grace provided in his Societies.

John Wesley spent six weeks in the Newcastle area on his third visit there in 1743. He visited the sick, organised and counselled the classes and preached on many occasions, including in what he called the 'shell' of the new 'Methodist' Preaching House that was being built. He also preached in villages around Newcastle and his experiences in Tanfield confirmed some of his evangelistic strategies. He complained that here, and in other places in England, there had been instances of evangelistic preaching that had been harmful. Because those spiritually awakened had not been organised into any kind of fellowship for follow-up counsel and spiritual encouragement, most of them had fallen away. Wesley commented: 'I am more and more convinced that the devil himself desires nothing more than this, that the people of any place should be half-awakened and then left to themselves to fall asleep again. Therefore I determine, by the grace of God, not to strike one stroke in any place where I cannot follow the blow.'[219] Wesley was convinced that just as gospel preaching was required to bring people to saving faith in Christ, it was no less necessary to organise

---

[218] John Wesley, *Works [BE]*, Vol. 9, pp.68-75.
[219] John Wesley, *Works [BE]*, Vol. 19, p.318.

them together for regular and systematic Bible teaching, spiritual edification, mutual encouragement, and, when necessary, discipline and correction. John Wesley, ever the practical theologian, took no less pains in organising the spiritual institutions that characterised his 'Methodism' than he did in his constant rounds of evangelistic preaching.

An observation that Wesley made while in Newcastle sheds light on how he decided where he should go to preach. Although his *Journal* indicates that in fifty years of itinerant evangelism he visited a very large number of both rural and urban areas in England, clearly he could not possibly visit every village and every town. How did he decide where to go? Riding back one evening to Newcastle he noted the mining village of Chowden. Already in the Newcastle area he had preached in many of the nearby towns and he recorded his particular delight on hearing that not only had people gathered to hear him from the surrounding areas but, in particular, from, 'all the neighbouring pits.' Wesley had noted that there was always a ready response to his preaching from the miners and their families. When he heard that the village of Chowden consisted of colliers only, he resolved to 'preach there as soon as possible, for these are sinners, and need repentance.'[220] Of course Wesley didn't mean that miners were necessarily more sinful than the other citizens of England, but he knew that in these mining villages, from Durham to Cornwall, there were thousands of his fellow-country men and women just 'ripe for the gospel.'

In June 1744 John Wesley, with his brother Charles, convened the first Conference of his preachers in London. The purpose was to review the progress of the 'Methodist' revival work across the country, discuss some theological and doctrinal questions that had arisen and make plans for both the expansion and consolidation of the work. The Conference became an annual event and its particular responsibility was the stationing of the preachers. John Wesley was already employing full-time, itinerant lay preachers and they were appointed

---

[220] John Wesley, *Works [BE],* Vol. 19, p.316.

to specific geographical areas known as 'circuits.' They were responsible for taking care of all the Societies in the circuit and Wesley expected them to exercise both pastoral care for those already in attendance and continued evangelistic ministry among the unawakened. The advice he gave to his preachers was embodied in his own non-stop itinerancy, leadership and overall responsibility for the rapidly-expanding Methodist movement.

> You have nothing to do but to save souls. Therefore spend and be spent in this work. And go always, not only to those that want you, but to those that want you most. Observe: It is not your business to preach so many times, and to take care of this or that society; but to save as many souls as you can; to bring as many sinners as you possibly can to repentance, and with all your power to build them up in that holiness without which they cannot see the Lord.[221]

By the middle of the 1740's, John Wesley had established most of the practices and institutions that would characterise the advance and consolidation of Methodism to the end of his life. From the very first beginnings of this work in London and Bristol, it was evident that John Wesley was no 'hit and run' evangelist. In observing many good practices among the Moravians, in consultation with his friends, and in his day-to-day, first-hand experiences of the revival, he evolved a strategy that would consolidate and preserve the work in his lifetime and beyond. The central pillar of this Methodist edifice was gospel preaching. John Wesley was unashamedly and apparently untiringly a gospel preacher. It is estimated that he travelled some one third million of miles on the roads of Britain for fifty years and preached approximately forty-five thousand times. Until Charles Wesley married in 1749, he, too, was as busy and as industrious as John, in itinerant evangelism. Then John Wesley began to select and appoint his travelling preachers and by his death more than three hundred of these were stationed across the circuits of England, Ireland and Scotland.

---

[221] John Wesley, 'Large Minutes', 1753, 12 Rules of a Helper, no. 11, *Works [BE]*, Vol. 10, p.854.

While itinerant preaching was central to John Wesley's work, he took no less care in organising for the spiritual oversight of his people. From the beginning all serious enquirers after 'the way of salvation' were enrolled in the local Societies, and then appointed to Bands and Classes as appropriate. Other 'Methodist' means of grace were also instituted, such as Quarterly Meetings, Watch-night Services and Love feasts. All this was in addition to Wesley's constant counsel to his people, to be regular in attendance at their parish church. Wesley's concern for the poor was early in evidence. He established an orphanage in Newcastle and schools in Kingswood. He opened a free dispensary in London and set up a loan fund, mostly from his own meagre income, so that poor people could borrow small amounts of money income free. John Wesley's life-long devotion to helping the poor was not just a minor part of his evangelistic enterprise. In his *Journal* for November 17, 1759, he wrote.

> I spent an hour agreeably and profitably with Sir Charles and Lady Hotham. It is well a few of the rich and noble are called. Oh that God would increase their number! But I should rejoice (were it the will of God), if it were done by the ministry of others. If I might choose, I should still, as I have done hitherto, preach the gospel to the poor.[222]

In addition to all this planning, organisation and network of spiritual care and accountability that stretched across the country, John Wesley had begun a publishing enterprise on behalf of the revival that would continue unabated till his death. As well as his journals and letters and sermons, he wrote and published theological treatises, fifty volumes of his extracts in the, *Christian Library*, apologias for the Christian faith in general and Methodism in particular, *Explanatory Notes,* on both Testaments, many volumes of his brother Charles' hymns, and much, much else. This huge publishing project, which amounted in total to some four hundred items, was another indication that John Wesley made every possible attempt to promote, extend and consolidate the 'Methodism' over which he believed God had appointed him leader.

---

[222] John Wesley, *Works [BE],* Vol. 21, p.233.

For the fifty-one years following his first open-air sermon in Bristol in 1739, John Wesley was, first and foremost, a preacher and an evangelist. That this remarkable ministry was launched by the experience of the 'warmed heart' on May 24, 1738, surely needs no verification, nor that the Spirit of the Lord rested on John Wesley in a very large measure. For half a century he travelled and preached in an itinerant ministry that has few, if any exact parallels, in the history of Christ's Church. In view of his constant gospel proclamation over the decades, it is surely a relevant question to ask – what kind of preacher was John Wesley? Can we learn anything about the content of his sermons, in what style they were delivered, and how did he sustain his preaching across so many years?

Among Wesley's publications were his many sermons, begun in 1746 under the title, *Sermons on Several Occasions*. He published other sermons singly and many were included among the contents of his monthly publication begun in 1778 the, *Arminian Magazine*. Altogether he published more than one hundred and forty sermons. Four of these were his university sermons, including, *The Circumcision of the Heart*, and, *Salvation by Faith*. All these published sermons show the signs of being carefully written, logically developed in argument, and freely sprinkled with Greek and Latin citations and quotations from English classical authors. The theological argumentation is frequently both deep and complex and often assumes more than just a cursory knowledge of Scripture and Christian theology. The question immediately suggested by reading almost any selection of these sermons is – how did the mostly-unchurched common people of 18th century England understand and respond in very large numbers to these often 'heavy' theological sermons?

The answer is – they didn't! John Wesley deliberately prepared these sermons for a reading public, and both in style and partly in content, they were distinctly different from the evangelistic sermons he preached daily across the country. Among the papers that Wesley left behind him was a memorandum entitled, *Sermon Register*. Commencing in January 1747, and running through until 1761, it is a careful record of where and from what Scripture text, Wesley preached in these fourteen years. The *Register* records the year, the date and the Scripture passage from which Wesley preached. In quite a number of places the Register gives information on a location where Wesley preached that is not included in his *Journal*. The most important information emerges when the Scripture texts given in this *Register* are compared with the texts used in the published sermons. Although there are some overlaps, they are almost two different lists. This means that while John Wesley wrote and published scores of sermons from the text given, he preached thousands of times from another set of favourite texts. The texts in the *Register*, and the favourite ones appear over and over again, were the Biblical passages from which John Wesley preached evangelistically, in a direct, impassioned style meant to bring his hearers to salvation. Eye-witness accounts speak of the illustrations he employed, in contrast to the published sermons which are almost wholly without illustrations. While the general content of all Wesley's sermons, written or preached, would not have differed much, the purposes of the two sermons collections were quite different. The published sermons were intended for those who could read, and while the evangelistic content is not entirely absent, the main purpose was to inform those who wanted to know what the Methodists believed, and provide a standard by which Methodist theology could be measured. The purpose of the sermons indicated by the *Register* was to make a direct evangelistic appeal, mostly out-of-doors, to the thousands of people who gathered to hear John Wesley. This preaching was carried on mainly in fields, cross roads, mining and rural areas, the villages, and, especially, the rapidly expanding cities of England's Industrial Revolution, like Manchester, Leeds and Birmingham.

The 'field preaching,' as Wesley called it, that he commenced in Bristol in April 1739, was to become the main thrust of his ministry for the next fifty-one years. In spite of his unflagging commitment to this kind of evangelism for so long, he was candid enough to admit that it was indeed 'a burden' given to him by the Lord. Preaching in Durham in June 1759, he commented that the number of people hearing him in the open air was double the number that the preaching house could contain. 'What marvel the devil does not love field-preaching! Neither do I: I love a commodious room, a soft cushion, a handsome pulpit. But where is my zeal, if I do not trample all these under foot in order to save one more soul.'[223]

From the very beginning of his itinerary, Wesley faced strong and persistent criticism from the Anglican clergy. They were not only opposed to the 'unorthodoxy' of field-preaching as such, but they objected to what they called Wesley's 'trespassing' into their parishes. When Wesley was summoned by Bishop Joseph Butler in August 1739, to explain what he was doing in Bristol, the learned prelate gave him advice. 'You have no business here; you are not commissioned to preach in this diocese, therefore I advise you to go hence.'[224] Believing he had the Lord's business to do in Bristol, Wesley replied.

> *My business on earth is to do what good I can.... A dispensation of the gospel is committed to me, and woe is me if I preach not the gospel... If I should be convinced that I could advance the glory of God and the salvation of souls in any other place more than in Bristol, in that hour, by God's help, I will go hence, which till then I may not do.*[225]

'My business on earth,' 'a dispensation of the gospel,' 'the glory of God,' 'the salvation of souls.' These telling phrases reveal a preacher who believes he has a commission from God and is totally committed to fulfilling that commission, even if that means offending a bishop in his Church.

In October that year, his elder brother, the Revd. Samuel Wesley, headmaster in Blundell's School in Tiverton, remonstrated with John that he should give up extempore preaching and extempore prayers and restrict his preaching to within 'consecrated walls.' John replied in kind.

---

[223] John Wesley, *Works [BE],* Vol. 21, p.203.
[224] John Wesley, *Journal*, Vol. 2, p.257, footnote.
[225] John Wesley, *Journal*, Vol. 2, p.257, footnote.

> How is it that you can't praise God for saving so many souls from death... unless he will begin this work from within 'consecrated walls'?... You cannot, indeed you cannot, confine the most high within temples made with hands. I do not despise them, any more than you do. But I rejoice to find that God is everywhere. I love the rights and ceremonies of the Church. But I see, well pleased, that our great Lord can work without them. And howsoever and wheresoever a sinner is converted from the error of his ways, nay, and by whomsoever, I therein rejoice, yea, and will rejoice.[226]

When a former member of the Oxford 'Holy Club' complained to Wesley that he was trespassing in other men's parishes, Wesley made a vigorous defence of his actions.

> On scriptural principles I do not think it hard to justify whatever I do. God in Scripture commands me, according to my power, to instruct the ignorant, reform the wicked, confirm the virtuous. Man forbids me to do this in another's parish; that is, in effect, to do it at all. Whom, then, shall I hear, God or man?.... Suffer me now to tell you my principles in this matter. I look upon all the world as my parish; thus far I mean, that in whatever part of I am, I judge it meet, right and my bounden duty to declare unto all that are willing to hear, the glad tidings of salvation. This is the work I know God has called me to do, and sure I am that His blessing attends it.... Blessed be God, I enjoy the reproach of Christ... If any man tell you there is a new way of following Christ, he is a liar and the truth is not in him.[227]

John Wesley was to discover that he would need repeatedly to explain and defend his evangelistic principles, especially to critical churchmen. In the 1740's he conducted a three-year correspondence with a 'John Smith.' Smith, whatever his real identity, was clearly a churchman, perhaps even holding a bishop's office, well versed in the laws and constitution of the Established Church – and he was not at all

---

[226] John Wesley, *Works [BE],* Vol. 25, pp.694, 695.
[227] John Wesley, *Works [BE],* Vol. 25, pp.615-617.

happy with Wesley's itinerant evangelism. Again Wesley was courteous but firm.

> Wherever I see one or a thousand men running into hell, be it in England, Ireland, or France, yea, in Europe, Asia, Africa, or America, I will stop them if I can: as a minister of Christ, I will beseech them in His name to turn back and be reconciled to God. Were I to do otherwise, were I to let any soul drop into the pit whom I might have saved from everlasting burnings, I am not satisfied God would accept my plea, 'Lord, he was not of my parish.'[228]

There is, then, the clearest evidence that John Wesley's remarkable half-century of itinerant evangelism began in Bristol that Monday afternoon in April 1739 when, in his own words, he consented to be 'more vile.' When John began to appoint laymen as preachers and send them out into the circuits he had devised, he knew exactly what their business was and what kind of men they needed to be. To one of them, Alexander Mather, Wesley wrote memorable words.

> The danger of ruin to Methodism is this. Our preachers, many of them, are fallen. They are not spiritual. They are not alive to God. They are soft, enervated, fearful of shame, toil, hardships.... Give me one hundred preachers who fear nothing but sin and desire nothing but God and I care not a straw whether they be clergymen or laymen, such alone will shake the gates of hell and set up the kingdom of heaven upon earth.[229]

Wesley used the texts he had used and for fifty years he proclaimed the grace of God. These sermons were not preached from written outlines or notes but straight from the biblical text. In many places in his *Journal* Wesley describes what his preaching was meant to do. 'I offered the grace of God.' 'I there offered Christ.' 'I offered the redemption that is in Christ Jesus.' 'I proclaimed the Name of the Lord.' 'I proclaimed Christ crucified.' 'I proclaimed free salvation.' 'I declared the free grace of God.' 'I exhorted the wicked to forsake his

---

[228] John Wesley, *Works*, *[BE]*, Vol. 26, p.291.
[229] John Wesley, *Letters*, Vol. 6, p.272.

way.' 'I began to call sinners to repentance.' This was soul-saving preaching and the sermons had anecdotes, illustrations and stories that the common people could easily understand. Wesley spoke from his heart in plain, pointed sentences that called sinners to repentance and directed them to faith in a crucified and risen Lord. These were evangelistic texts and they demanded a response. Arthur Wood comments.

> His was true Biblical preaching ... As an evangelist, he knew that his main task was to persuade man. However faithfully the message might be delivered, he realised it was not enough to leave there. The appeal had to be pressed home in a personal manner, so that every hearer was left feeling that the protective covering of neutrality and indifference had been stripped off, and that a decisive moment had arrived.[230]

In the next fifty years this was his main occupation and field-preaching his preeminent style. In the out-of-doors in the open field, on street corners, at factory gates, he met the people in congregations larger than church buildings could contain. Though often ridiculed and maligned because of his preaching policy, Wesley never quit. What difference did it make that the sophisticated clergymen of his day scorned him? God was using his methods to awaken lost souls to their privileges of grace and that was all that mattered. Wesley was so committed to taking the gospel to the people that he grew impatient when prevented by inclement weather. He wrote to James Rea in 1766. 'Preach abroad – if ever you would do good. It is the cooping yourselves up in rooms that has damped the work of God, which never was and never will be carried on to any purpose without going out into the highways and hedges and compelling poor sinners to come in.'[231]

Robert Coleman is of the opinion that we must look to John Wesley to get the larger picture.

> What is ignored is that Wesley's conciliar principle applied only to peripheral matters – like modes of baptism or

---

[230] Arthur Wood, *The Burning Heart*, p.157.
[231] John Wesley, *Letters*, Vol. 5, p.23.

ecclesiastical forms of government – and was never intended to excuse deviation from basic biblical revelation. This deposit of non-negotiable truth included such foundational doctrines as original sin; the Saviour's virgin birth; his vicarious blood atonement; the bodily resurrection; Christ's ascension, reign, and triumphant return; and the judgment fully to imagine that the church today can produce the fruits of the Gospel without similar doctrinal integrity. There can be go genuine witness nor growth in spiritual experience, if we do not believe the Bible message.[232]

Perhaps there is a clue to Wesley's destiny to be found much earlier than that. On September 19, 1731, John Wesley preached in Christ Church Cathedral, Oxford, on the occasion of an ordination service. The leader of the Oxford 'Holy Club' chose as his theme, *The Wisdom of Winning Souls,* and took his text from Proverbs 11:30.

> In a place where philosophy, or the love of wisdom is so universally professed and so carefully cultivated, where so many are obliged by their office to study and practise this particular sort of wisdom... it can't but be highly proper to make that wisdom the subject of our consideration.... 'He that winneth souls is wise.' He that draws them from vice to virtue, from rebellion against God to obedience, that recovers them from darkness and the shadow of death to the way of light and peace... he is wise indeed![233]

Near the end of the sermon, in a passage arguing that soul-winning must not be restricted to full-time clergy, Wesley was near-prophetic about his later life's work and Methodism when he declared: 'Here a general commission is given to all the servants of Christ to tread in his steps, to do what in them lies in their several stations to save the souls for whom Christ died.... What Scripture denies any man the power of beseeching others, for Christ's sake, to be reconciled to God?'[234]

---

[232] Robert Coleman, *Nothing To Do But To Save Souls*, p. 30.
[233] John Wesley, *Works [BE],* Vol. 4, pp.306, 307.
[234] John Wesley, *Works [BE],* Vol. 4, p.316.

Bibliography

Henry Bett, *The Spirit of Methodism,* Oxford Press, 1927.

Gerald Bray, *Biblicial Interpretation: Past and Present*, London, 1987.

Gilbert Burnet, *An Exposition of the Thirty-Nine Articles of the Church of England,* 1699.

The Homilies, Not known.

Thomas Jackson, *The Life of Charles Wesley,* 2 Vols. 1841.

Scott J. Jones, *John Wesley's Conception and Use of Scripture,* Kingswood Books, Nashville, Tennessee, 1995.

Henry R. McAdoo, *The Spirit of Anglicanism,* London, 1965.

Kenneth G. C. Newport, *The Sermons of Charles Wesley*, Oxford, 2001.

Paul Taylor and H. Mellor, 'Luther's Principles of Biblical Interpretation,' *Travelling Man,* Moorleys Print and Publishing, Ilkeston, 1994.

Albert Outler, *John Wesley,* Oxford, 1964.

John Pearson, *An Exposition of the Creed,* 1823.

Charles Wesley, *The Journal of Charles Wesley,* Vols. 1 and 2. Kingswood Books, Nashville, Tennessee, 2008.

John Wesley, *The Works of John Wesley,* 14 vols. Nazarene Publishing House, Kansas City, Missouri, 1955.

The Bicentennial Edition of the Works of John Wesley, 21 Vols. Abington Press, 1989 – 2019, Nashville, Tennessee.

The Letters of the Rev. John Wesley, 8 Vols. Edited by John Telford, Epworth Press, London, 1931.

The Journal of the Rev. John Wesley, 8 Vols. Edited by Nehemiah Curnoch, Epworth Press, London, 1938.

George Allan Turner, *The More Excellent Way: A Scriptural Basis of the Wesleyan Message*, Winone Lake, 1952.

John Wesley, *Explanatory Notes upon the New Testament*, London, Wesleyan Methodist Book Room, Paternoster Row.

John Wesley, *Explanatory Notes upon the Old Testament*, Bristol, 1765.

Arthur Skevington Wood, *The Burning Heart,* Exeter, The Paternoster Press, 1967.

Books by Revd Dr Herbert Boyd McGonigle

William Cooke on Entire Sanctification, Beacon Hill Press, Kansas City, Missouri, 1978.

The Arminianism of John Wesley, Moorleys Print & Publishing, Ilkeston, Derbyshire, 1988.

John Wesley and the Moravians, Moorleys Print & Publishing, Ilkeston, Derbyshire, 1995.

John Wesley's Doctrine of Prevenient Grace, Moorleys Print & Publishing, Ilkeston, Derbyshire, 1995.

Scriptural Holiness: The Wesleyan Distinctive, Moorleys Print & Publishing, Ilkeston, Derbyshire, 1995.

Sufficient Saving Grace: John Wesley's Evangelical Arminianism, 350 pages, Paternoster Publishing, Carlisle, Cumbria, 2001.

To God Be The Glory: The Killadeas Convention 1952-2002, Moorleys Print & Publishing, Ilkeston, Derbyshire, 2002.

John Wesley's Arminian Theology: An Introduction, Moorleys Print & Publishing, Ilkeston, Derbyshire, 2005.

A Burning and a Shining Light: The Life and Ministry of William Bramwell, Moorleys Print & Publishing, Ilkeston, Derbyshire, 2009.

Christianity or Deism? John Wesley's Response to John Taylor's Denial of the Doctrine of Original Sin, Moorleys Print & Publishing, Ilkeston, Derbyshire, 2012.

John Wesley: Exemplar of the Catholic Spirit, Moorleys Print & Publishing, Ilkeston, Derbyshire, 2014.

Charles Wesley: For All, For All My Saviour Died, Moorleys Print & Publishing, Ilkeston, Derbyshire, 2014.

John Wesley: The Death of Christ, Moorleys Print & Publishing, Ilkeston, Derbyshire, 2014.

Epworth: The Cradle of Methodism, Moorleys Print & Publishing, Ilkeston, Derbyshire, 2014.

John Wesley: Doctrine of Final Judgement, Moorleys Print & Publishing, Ilkeston, Derbyshire, 2015.

Thomas Walsh: Saint and Scholar, Moorleys Print & Publishing, Ilkeston, Derbyshire, 2015.

Our Story: Autobiographical thoughts from the pen of Revd. Dr. Herbert B. McGonigle, Nazarene Theological College Archives, Manchester, 2015.

Dr. Adam Clarke: Methodist Preacher and Scholar, Moorleys Print & Publishing, Ilkeston, Derbyshire, 2015.

Gideon Ouseley: Methodist Preacher and Biblical Scholar, Moorleys Print & Publishing, Ilkeston, Derbyshire, 2015.

Thomas Cook: Evangelist and Saint, Moorleys Print & Publishing, Ilkeston, Derbyshire, 2016.

The Methodist Pentecost, 1758-1763, Moorleys Print & Publishing, Ilkeston, Derbyshire, 2016.

John Fletcher, Methodist Saint and Scholar, Moorleys Print & Publishing, Ilkeston, Derbyshire, 2016.

An Appreciation of Revd. Dr. John Henry Jowett's Heaven's Hallelujah, Moorleys Print & Publishing, Ilkeston, Derbyshire, 2016.

General William Booth, Moorleys Print & Publishing, Ilkeston, Derbyshire, 2016.

John Wesley on The Great Salvation, Moorleys Print & Publishing, Ilkeston, Derbyshire, 2017.

Samuel Chadwick: Preacher and Evangelist, Moorleys Print & Publishing, Ilkeston, Derbyshire, 2017.

Francis William Crossley, Moorleys Print & Publishing, Ilkeston, Derbyshire, 2018.

Dr. Alexander Maclaren: Preacher and Expositor, Moorleys Print & Publishing, Ilkeston, Derbyshire, 2018.

Herbert and Jeanne McGonigle: Our Story, Moorleys Print & Publishing, Ilkeston, Derbyshire, 2018.

Through the Year with John and Charles Wesley, Moorleys Print & Publishing, Ilkeston, Derbyshire, 2019.